THE
END
OF THE
AGE

THE COUNTDOWN
HAS BEGUN

STUDY GUIDE | TWELVE LESSONS

JOHN HAGEE

HarperChristian
Resources

The End of the Age Study Guide
© 2021 by John Hagee

Requests for information should be addressed to:
HarperChristian Resources, 3900 Sparks Dr. SE, Grand Rapids, Michigan 49546

ISBN 978-0-310-14027-6 (softcover)
ISBN 978-0-310-14028-3 (ebook)

HarperChristian Resources titles may be purchased in bulk for church, business, fundraising, or ministry use. For information, please e-mail ResourceSpecialist@ChurchSource.com.

First Printing February 2022 / Printed in the United States of America

CONTENTS

11:50 PM

The End of the Age

Jesus came and spoke to them, saying . . . "Lo, I am with you always, even to the end of the age."

Matthew 28:18, 20

In many ways, the end of the world as we know it is here. It arrived neither with a bang nor a whimper but is occurring in stages clearly set forth in God's Word. . . . The new age is about to be born, but the most severe contractions are just before us.

From Chapter 1 of *The End of the Age*

The headline was both stark and serious: "It Is 100 Seconds to Midnight." On January 27, 2021, the *Bulletin of the Atomic Scientists* updated their famous Doomsday Clock to 11:58:20, matching the highest level to which that clock had ever counted.

Founded in 1945 by scientists from the Manhattan Project, to include Albert Einstein, the *Bulletin*'s Doomsday Clock offers a compelling visual to illustrate the different threats currently affecting humanity and our planet. Midnight on that clock represents total destruction of the world and annihilation of the human species.

To offer some context, the clock's first setting was at 11:53:00 in 1947, just after the end of the second World War. At the start of the Cold War in 1953, the clock shifted to 11:57:00. In 1991—a period of relative safety and prosperity—the clock moved all the way back to 11:43:00. Since 2015, the Doomsday Clock has been set at "three minutes to midnight" or later.

From pastors to politicians and beyond, people have been predicting the end of the world as we know it for thousands of years. It's part of human nature to imagine how everything might come crashing down.

Yet there seems to be a particular urgency in the prophetic doom-saying of our modern world. A greater sense of somberness exists, perhaps because end-of-the-world scenarios have gone from Hollywood fodder to real life. We have witnessed firsthand the tension of standoffs between nuclear-armed nations. We've lived through the pressure of a pandemic. We are constantly bombarded by cataclysmic doomsday theories of climate change and the increasing chaos of civil unrest.

Rather than feeling farfetched, the End of the Age now seems almost a given. A matter of *when* rather than *if*. Of course, none of this is news to students of biblical prophecy. The pages of God's Word offer a window into "the end of the age" (Matthew 13:49).

The goal of this study guide is to look through that window together—not necessarily to make specific predictions about people and places, but to gain wisdom and perspective from the Author. In the process, we will see what God has in store for the future so that we can remain ready, speak boldly, and live faithfully.

Explore the Scripture

When we hear the term *biblical prophecy*, we might think first of the book of Revelation. There is a good reason for this. Revelation is filled almost exclusively with prophetic passages and apocalyptic visions. However, in my experience, nowhere in Scripture is God's prophetic plan more fully illustrated—or more accurately described—than in the book of Daniel. Situated among the Major Prophets, Daniel portrays several visions in which the future of the world is revealed, and many of these insights have been fulfilled with 100 percent accuracy.

As we begin our study of the End of the Age, I want to look at a pivotal moment not only for Daniel as a young man and future prophet but also for King Nebuchadnezzar—the most powerful man in the world during his day. It happened one night when Nebuchadnezzar had a dream. This was not a normal dream but a prophetic vision that disturbed him. The king called together all the wise men and sorcerers of his court and demanded they reveal to him not only the meaning of the dream but also the dream itself. In fact, Nebuchadnezzar was so desperate for an accurate interpretation that he made a proclamation: if the wise men and sorcerers could not reveal both the contents and the meaning of the dream, they would all be executed.

The wise men answered with the truth: "There is not a man on earth who can tell the king's matter. . . . There is no other who can tell it to the king except the gods, whose dwelling is not with flesh" Daniel 2:10–11)

Then Daniel entered the scene. He was a recent captive from the little province of Israel. He approached the king with confidence and humility and spoke the following:

> [31] *"You, O king, were watching; and behold, a great image! This great image, whose splendor was excellent, stood before you; and its form was awesome.* [32] *This image's head was of fine gold, its chest and arms of silver, its belly and thighs of bronze,* [33] *its legs of iron, its feet partly of iron and partly of clay.* [34] *You watched while a stone was cut out without hands, which struck the image on its feet of iron and clay, and broke them in pieces.* [35] *Then the iron, the clay, the bronze, the silver, and the gold were crushed together, and became like chaff from the summer threshing floors; the wind carried them away so that no trace of them was found. And the stone that struck the image became a great mountain and filled the whole earth.*
>
> [36] *"This is the dream. Now we will tell the interpretation of it before the king.* [37] *You, O king, are a king of kings. For the God of heaven has given you a kingdom, power, strength, and glory;* [38] *and wherever the children of men dwell, or the beasts of the field and the birds of the heaven, He has given them into your hand, and has*

made you ruler over them all—you are this head of gold. [39] But after you shall arise another kingdom inferior to yours; then another, a third kingdom of bronze, which shall rule over all the earth. [40] And the fourth kingdom shall be as strong as iron, inasmuch as iron breaks in pieces and shatters everything; and like iron that crushes, that kingdom will break in pieces and crush all the others. [41] Whereas you saw the feet and toes, partly of potter's clay and partly of iron, the kingdom shall be divided; yet the strength of the iron shall be in it, just as you saw the iron mixed with ceramic clay. [42] And as the toes of the feet were partly of iron and partly of clay, so the kingdom shall be partly strong and partly fragile. [43] As you saw iron mixed with ceramic clay, they will mingle with the seed of men; but they will not adhere to one another, just as iron does not mix with clay. [44] And in the days of these kings the God of heaven will set up a kingdom which shall never be destroyed; and the kingdom shall not be left to other people; it shall break in pieces and consume all these kingdoms, and it shall stand forever. [45] Inasmuch as you saw that the stone was cut out of the mountain without hands, and that it broke in pieces the iron, the bronze, the clay, the silver, and the gold—the great God has made known to the king what will come to pass after this. The dream is certain, and its interpretation is sure."

(DANIEL 2:31–45)

What are your first reactions to Nebuchadnezzar's dream (see verses 31–35)? What stands out as you read it?

What do the statue's different materials communicate?

- Gold:

- Silver:

- Bronze:

- Iron and clay:

What seems significant about the different features emphasized within the statue?

- Head:

- Chest:

- Belly and thighs:

- Feet:

How would you summarize or restate Daniel's interpretation of the vision (see verses 37–45)?

What are the different phrases that Daniel used to describe God throughout these verses? What do those names and titles communicate?

Daniel described God's kingdom manifest on earth in verses 44–45. What specific claims did Daniel make regarding that kingdom?

Nebuchadnezzar wasn't the only one who was given a vision in the book of Daniel. Daniel himself received prophetic insight into the future through a dream that complemented what he had described to the king.

> [2] *Daniel spoke, saying, "I saw in my vision by night, and behold, the four winds of heaven were stirring up the Great Sea.* [3] *And four great beasts came up from the sea, each different from the other.* [4] *The first was like a lion, and had eagle's wings. I watched till its wings were plucked off, and it was lifted up from the earth and made to stand on two feet like a man, and a man's heart was given to it.*
>
> [5] *"And suddenly another beast, a second, like a bear. It was raised up on one side, and had three ribs in its mouth between its teeth. And they said thus to it: 'Arise, devour much flesh!'*

⁶ *"After this I looked, and there was another, like a leopard, which had on its back four wings of a bird. The beast also had four heads, and dominion was given to it.*

⁷ *"After this I saw in the night visions, and behold, a fourth beast, dreadful and terrible, exceedingly strong. It had huge iron teeth; it was devouring, breaking in pieces, and trampling the residue with its feet. It was different from all the beasts that were before it, and it had ten horns.* ⁸ *I was considering the horns, and there was another horn, a little one, coming up among them, before whom three of the first horns were plucked out by the roots. And there, in this horn, were eyes like the eyes of a man, and a mouth speaking pompous words.*

(DANIEL 7:2–8)

What strikes you as most interesting about Daniel's dream? Why?

How do the four beasts of Daniel's dream correspond to the statue in Nebuchadnezzar's dream?

- The Lion

- The Bear

- The Leopard

- The Terrible Beast

How do both visions highlight God's sovereignty? His power?

Reflect on the Scripture

The book of Daniel reflected the future, and history proved it true. The four beasts mentioned in Daniel's vision have a direct, definitive, provable connection to four historical kingdoms. Importantly, those beasts also correspond with the four pieces of the statue in Nebuchadnezzar's vision—the head, chest, belly/thighs, and feet.

The first beast was like a lion with the wings of an eagle. This is the exact representation of the Babylonian national symbol. Nebuchadnezzar had risen to staggering heights of accomplishment and took pride in his success, but God struck him down in a supernatural display of divine power. The king lost his mind and actually ate grass like an ox for seven years, after which God restored his sanity. He returned to his kingdom with the heart "of a man" and a new appreciation for the power of Daniel's God (see Daniel 4).

The second beast, a lopsided bear, represents the Medo-Persian Empire. (The beast was lopsided because the Medes were more prominent than the Persians.) The three ribs in the bear's mouth graphically illustrate the three prominent conquests of the empire: (1) Lydia in 546 BCE, (2) Babylon in 539 BCE, and (3) Egypt in 525 BCE. A succession of kings ruled this empire, including King Ahasuerus (Xerxes) of the book of Esther. The Persian ruler Artaxerxes was king during Nehemiah's royal service.

The third beast, the leopard with four wings and four heads, represents Greece under Alexander the Great. The leopard is a swift animal, symbolizing the blinding speed with which Alexander's military attacked its enemies. At his death, Alexander's four leading generals divided his kingdom into four separate regions—thus the leopard's four wings and four heads.

The frightening fourth beast, more terrifying than its predecessors, represents the Roman Empire and the final form of Gentile power on earth. The ten horns of Daniel's dream correspond to the ten toes in Nebuchadnezzar's dream. The horns represent ten kings or leaders who will lead nations (a European federation) that will rise from the ashes of the Roman Empire.

How do these historical events indicate that God's Word is true and reliable?

Using the following scale, how would you rate your level of confidence when it comes to understanding and applying biblical prophecy?

1	2	3	4	5	6	7	8	9	10
	(Low confidence)						(High confidence)		

How do you think that you could benefit through a greater understanding of biblical prophecy?

What are some limits to what biblical prophecy can teach or reveal?

As a follower of Jesus, what are practical steps that you can take to avoid false teaching or potential overreaching when it comes to connecting biblical prophecy with current events?

Act in Faith

In the classic movie *Back to the Future II*, the young protagonist Marty McFly is taken thirty years into the future by his friend Doc, the inventor of a time machine. Once their mission in the future is complete, Marty attempts to benefit financially by purchasing a book of sports "history" that—if brought back to the past—would allow the young man to make millions of dollars through gambling. In the end, Marty's plan backfires. Indeed, the entire trilogy of *Back to the Future* movies serves as a cautionary tale against allowing the pressure of the future (or the past) to prevent one from truly living in and experiencing the present.

There is a similar dynamic that comes into play with biblical prophecy. Many people believe that prophecy exists to give Christians a leg up—to benefit us somehow through advanced knowledge. Instead, biblical prophecy exists for three primary reasons:

1. **To boost our faith.** When we see prophetic events coming true—such as the four kingdoms prophesied in the book of Daniel—it builds our trust in the reliability of God's Word.

2. **To glorify God.** The more we witness God's sovereignty and power expressed through biblical prophecy, the more we revere and praise Him as God.

3. **To help us stand during times of trouble.** Much of biblical prophecy points forward to moments of extreme tribulation and distress. The End of the Age will not be a pleasant period—especially for disciples of Christ. Yet following God's roadmap for the future will allow us to not simply endure the difficult seasons but also to stand as witnesses for God's kingdom both in and through them.

As we make our way through this study, we will explore all three of these benefits in greater detail. At the end of each lesson, we will focus especially on the opportunities we have to stand for Christ today—right at this moment.

What is one step you can take this week to demonstrate your trust in God's sovereignty and power?

What is one step you can take this week to demonstrate your belief in the truth of God's Word?

As you close this lesson, read aloud the conclusion of Daniel's vision:

13 I was watching in the night visions,
And behold, One like the Son of Man,
Coming with the clouds of heaven!
He came to the Ancient of Days,
And they brought Him near before Him.

14 Then to Him was given dominion and glory and a kingdom,
That all peoples, nations, and languages should serve Him.
His dominion is an everlasting dominion,
Which shall not pass away,
And His kingdom the one
Which shall not be destroyed.

(DANIEL 7:13–14)

Responsive Prayer: *Lord Jesus, I declare as Your disciple that You are the Ancient of Days. You alone have been given dominion and glory and an eternal kingdom that shall not pass away. Just as all peoples, nations, and languages will serve You, I choose here and now to serve You. Amen.*

11:51 PM

Messiah the Prince Enters Jerusalem

*And when He had come into Jerusalem, all the city was moved, saying,
"Who is this?"*

Matthew 21:10

*Jesus rode into Jerusalem as a man of peace on a humble donkey.
Christ came to Earth the first time as a sacrificial lamb to redeem the
world from sin . . . to bring a lasting spiritual peace between God and man.
And to accomplish this divine assignment, Jesus had to suffer and die.*

From Chapter 2 of *The End of the Age*

As we've already seen in lesson one, biblical prophecy is both highly accurate and specific. Daniel's prophecy of the four future kingdoms—Babylon, Medo-Persia, Greece, and Rome—has been proven through history to be filled with pertinent details and fulfilled in ways that leave no room for doubt.

We will see the same level of specificity and accuracy in this lesson as we examine Daniel's prophetic vision of the "seventy weeks"—and the precise ways those prophecies were confirmed by Jesus' triumphal entry into Jerusalem.

Explore the Scripture

It's interesting that Daniel received one of the most important prophetic visions in Scripture largely because he was a student of biblical prophecy. According to Daniel 9, the prophet "understood by the books the number of the years specified by the word of the LORD through Jeremiah the prophet, that He would accomplish seventy years in the desolations of Jerusalem" (verse 2).

Daniel was referring to Jeremiah 25:11–12, in which the weeping prophet had foretold that God's people would be taken as captives to Babylon and that their captivity would last seventy years. This period of time had almost come to an end. Therefore, Daniel prayed with great fervency that his people would walk rightly before God and that He would bring about the deliverance He had promised.

In response to this prayer, Daniel was once again visited by the angel Gabriel. "At the beginning of your supplications the command went out," said Gabriel, "and I have come to tell you, for you are greatly beloved; therefore consider the matter, and understand the vision" (Daniel 9:23). What followed was a vision that crystallizes God's prophetic plan for history:

> [24] *"Seventy weeks are determined*
> *For your people and for your holy city,*
> *To finish the transgression,*
> *To make an end of sins,*
> *To make reconciliation for iniquity,*
> *To bring in everlasting righteousness,*
> *To seal up vision and prophecy,*
> *And to anoint the Most Holy.*

25 *"Know therefore and understand,*
That from the going forth of the command
To restore and build Jerusalem
Until Messiah the Prince,
There shall be seven weeks and sixty-two weeks;
The street shall be built again, and the wall,
Even in troublesome times.

26 *"And after the sixty-two weeks*
Messiah shall be cut off, but not for Himself;
And the people of the prince who is to come
Shall destroy the city and the sanctuary.
The end of it shall be with a flood,
And till the end of the war desolations are determined.

27 *Then he shall confirm a covenant with many for one week;*
But in the middle of the week
He shall bring an end to sacrifice and offering.
And on the wing of abominations shall be one who makes desolate,
Even until the consummation, which is determined,
Is poured out on the desolate."

(DANIEL 9:24–27)

What are your initial reactions to this vision? What strikes you as especially important or noteworthy?

What can you say for certain about the "seventy weeks" based on these verses?

Which of the prophetic promises in these verses have already been fulfilled?

Which of the promises are yet to be fulfilled?

Daniel's vision specifically points forward to Jesus, whom he calls "Messiah the Prince" (verse 25). With the benefit of hindsight, we now understand that Daniel was highlighting Jesus' triumphal entry into the city of Jerusalem. In ancient days, it was common for rulers to enter large cities as part of a procession, with much pomp and ceremony designed to exalt that ruler in the eyes of the people. However, Jesus entered Jerusalem in a much different manner:

> ¹ *Now when they drew near Jerusalem, and came to Bethphage, at the Mount of Olives, then Jesus sent two disciples,* ² *saying to them, "Go into the village opposite you, and immediately you will find a donkey tied, and a colt with her. Loose them and bring them to Me.* ³ *And if anyone says anything to you, you shall say, 'The Lord has need of them,' and immediately he will send them."*
>
> ⁴ *All this was done that it might be fulfilled which was spoken by the prophet, saying:*
>
> > ⁵ *"Tell the daughter of Zion,*
> > *'Behold, your King is coming to you,*
> > *Lowly, and sitting on a donkey,*
> > *A colt, the foal of a donkey.' "*
>
> ⁶ *So the disciples went and did as Jesus commanded them.* ⁷ *They brought the donkey and the colt, laid their clothes on them, and set Him on them.* ⁸ *And a very great multitude spread their clothes on the road; others cut down branches from the trees and spread them on the road.* ⁹ *Then the multitudes who went before and those who followed cried out, saying:*

"Hosanna to the Son of David!
'Blessed is He who comes in the name of the Lord!'
Hosanna in the highest!"

[10] *And when He had come into Jerusalem, all the city was moved, saying,*
"Who is this?"
[11] *So the multitudes said, "This is Jesus, the prophet from Nazareth of Galilee."*

(MATTHEW 21:1–11)

Where do you see evidence from the text that this was an important moment in the life of Christ?

Where do you see evidence in the text that this moment was a fulfillment of prophecy?

What words would you use to describe Jesus in this moment?

Reflect on the Scripture

A key to understanding the prophecy given to Daniel is to understand the Seventy Weeks of Daniel 9:24. The Hebrew word for *seven* is *shabua*, meaning "a unit of measure."[1] It is similar to how we use the word *dozen*, which could signify a dozen groupings of anything. Daniel had been reading about the seventy years of exile in the writings of Jeremiah, and he thought of them as literal years. However, the Lord revealed through Gabriel that the Seventy Weeks refers to a specific period of time totaling "seventy sets of seven." In this case, the vision means seven times seventy years, for a total time period of 490 years.

God's angelic messenger further subdivided the Seventy Weeks into intervals, with each week representing seven years on the human calendar. The first segment totaled seven weeks (7 x 7, or 49 years), the second period equated to sixty-two weeks (62 x 7, or 434 years), and the final interval was one week (7 years). Here's where Daniel's vision becomes *incredibly* specific, *incredibly* accurate, and *incredibly* encouraging for all readers of God's Word. Look again at Daniel 9:25: "Know therefore and understand, that from the going forth of the command to restore and build Jerusalem until Messiah the Prince, there shall be seven weeks and sixty-two weeks."

The decree to rebuild Jerusalem— issued during the time of Nehemiah—was given in 445 BCE. For forty-nine years (the first unit of seven "weeks" of years), Nehemiah and his men labored to rebuild the wall, even during "troublesome times" (verse 25,) until the work was completed in 396 BCE. Next, Daniel prophesied that following an additional sixty-two week period (creating a total of sixty-nine "weeks" of years), the Messiah would be "cut off" (verse 26).

On the tenth day of Nisan in the year 32 CE, Jesus of Nazareth rode into Jerusalem to publicly offer Himself as Israel's suffering Messiah—what we know as the "triumphal entry." In the words of theologian Sir Robert Anderson, the interval between March 14, 445 BCE and April 6, 32 CE "contained exactly and to the very day [173,880] days, or seven times sixty-nine prophetic years of 360 days."[2] Jesus' triumphal entry fulfilled Daniel's prophecy to the *exact day*.

How would you describe the connection between Daniel's "seventy weeks" and Jesus' triumphal entry in Jerusalem?

How does Daniel's vision in 9:24–27 provide specific evidence for the accuracy of biblical prophecy?

The following are ten Old Testament prophecies concerning the coming of the Messiah. Look up the corresponding New Testament passage and record how the prophecy was fulfilled through the birth, life, death, and resurrection of Christ.[3]

Old Testament Prophecy	New Testament Fulfillment
Isaiah 7:14: *"Behold, the virgin shall conceive and bear a Son."*	Matthew 1:20:
Micah 5:2: *"But you, Bethlehem Ephrathah . . . out of you shall come forth to Me the One to be Ruler in Israel."*	Matthew 2:1–6:
Hosea 11:1: *"When Israel was a child, I loved him, and out of Egypt I called My son."*	Matthew 2:15:
Isaiah 35:5–6: *"Then the eyes of the blind shall be opened, and the ears of the deaf shall be unstopped. Then the lame shall leap like a deer, and the tongue of the dumb sing."*	Matthew 11:2–6:
Zechariah 9:9: *"Behold, your King is coming to you . . . lowly and riding on a donkey, a colt, the foal of a donkey."*	Matthew 21:4–10
Psalm 41:9: *"Even my own familiar friend in whom I trusted, who ate my bread, has lifted up his heel against me."*	John 13:18, 26:
Psalm 22:18: *"They divide My garments among them, and for My clothing they cast lots."*	Luke 23:34–35:

Old Testament Prophecy	New Testament Fulfillment
Psalm 34:20: *"He guards all his bones; not one of them is broken."*	John 19:33, 36:
Jonah 1:17: *"Jonah was in the belly of the fish three days and three nights."*	Matthew 12:40:
Isaiah 53:5: *"But He was wounded for our transgressions, He was bruised for our iniquities; the chastisement for our peace was upon Him, and by His stripes we are healed."*	Philippians 2:6–8:

How would you respond to someone who claimed that Jesus was not a historical person?

Act in Faith

To summarize what we've discussed in this lesson, Daniel's vision of the Seventy Weeks offers a prophetic timeline through which we can understand the events of history. Sixty-nine of those "weeks"—a total of 483 prophetic years—covered the period between Nehemiah's proclamation to rebuild the temple in Jerusalem to Jesus' triumphal entry into that city prior to His death and resurrection.

The final "week" from Daniel's vision refers to the seven years of the Great Tribulation, which we will cover in more detail in later lessons of this study guide. Notably, most biblical scholars agree that there is a gap between the sixty-ninth and seventieth weeks—what we could call a "Divine Intermission." During this period, Israel has been temporarily "sidetracked" while Christ continues to build His church and advance His kingdom through the Gentiles.

In essence, God has pressed "pause" on His prophetic clock in order to establish the church and spread the gospel to every tongue, tribe, and nation. When that goal has been completed, God will restart the prophetic clock, and the world will experience the awesome and terrible events of the Great Tribulation prior to the millennial reign of Christ.

One of the reasons why it's important to recognize this Divine Intermission is that we are currently living on the precipice of the End of the Age. The modern church exists to accomplish Christ's will and advance the gospel during this prophetic pause. This means that we have important work to do until God's clock begins turning once more.

In *Earth's Last Empire: The Final Game of Thrones,* I discuss the following regarding the gap, or intermission, between the sixty-ninth and seventieth years:

Why did the clock stop ticking, and when will it begin again?

Remember, the seventy weeks relate solely to God's dealings with the Jewish people—the church of Jesus Christ is nowhere mentioned. However, the New Testament church occupies that gap from the day of Pentecost (see Acts 2:1) until the Rapture of the church . . . (see 1 Corinthians 15:52).

What marked the beginning of the Church Age, when will it end, and when will the seventieth week begin? The Church was birthed at Pentecost, and its age will last until Christ raptures His bride into the third heaven—it is the Dispensation of Grace. . . .

Think of the Jewish nation as being placed on the sidetrack by God Himself, awaiting the arrival and fulfillment of the "Gentile Express" (see Romans 11:25). The temporary sidetracking of the Jewish nation has made space for the fast-tracking of the Gentile nation. This pause on the path to the ultimate redemption we all long for is God's grace in action and in no way violates His promise to the Jewish people.[4]

Based on this reading, how would you explain this "gap" in your own words—both what it is and why it is occurring?

Read again Jesus' Great Commission: "Go therefore and make disciples of all the nations, baptizing them in the name of the Father and of the Son and of the Holy Spirit, teaching them to observe all things that I have commanded you; and lo, I am with you always, even to the end of the age" (Matthew 18:18–20). Where do you have an opportunity this week to follow Jesus' commands in these verses?

What are some obstacles that have hindered or weakened your efforts for evangelism? How can you better overcome those obstacles?

Responsive Prayer: *Lord Jesus, I affirm that You are with me always. When I act for Your kingdom, I act in Your strength. When I teach Your Word, I teach what is true. When I baptize in Your name, I exercise Your authority. And when I make disciples for Your church, I obey Your will. Amen.*

NOTES
1. Bible Hub, s.v. "shabua," https://bibleapps.com/hebrew/7620. htm.
2. Robert Anderson, *The Coming Prince: The Last Great Monarch of Christendom* (London: Hodder & Stoughton, 1881), pp. 112–113.
3. See chapter 2 in *The End of the Age* for a list of fifty Old Testament prophecies that were fulfilled in Christ.
4. John Hagee, *Earth's Last Empire* (New York: Hachette Book Group, 2018, 2020).

11:52 PM

And Knowledge Shall Increase

But you, Daniel, shut up the words, and seal the book until the time of the end; many shall run to and fro, and knowledge shall increase.

Daniel 12:4

We have built a society upon the pillars of technology. . . . Like in the times of Babel, we have conveniently forgotten or deliberately ignored God's precepts and warnings in order to go our own way. But as the clock nears midnight, my friend, the birth pangs of the coming End of the Age are sending shock waves throughout civilization.

From Chapter 3 of *The End of the Age*

The COVID-19 pandemic that broke out in January 2020 resulted in the deaths of millions of people around the globe. Thankfully, hundreds of millions of people overcame the virus and were able to resume their lives.

Mildred Schappals was among that group. She contracted COVID-19 in May 2020 and recovered quickly. But what's remarkable is that Mildred was 102 years old at the time! In fact, Mildred Schappals is one of only a handful of people who defeated both COVID-19 and the Spanish Flu of 1918. (Mildred was ten months old when she contracted the Spanish Flu.)[1]

Surviving two pandemics across two centuries is certainly noteworthy. But it's also interesting to ponder everything that Mildred has experienced during her long and laudable life—especially in terms of the advances we have seen in the past hundred years. For instance, think of the technology associated with travel. Mildred has seen the world move from horses and buggies to automobiles—and to self-driving cars today. She witnessed the advent of commercial air travel, the arrival of space travel, and now the advent of commercial travel into space. She was born in a world where the vast majority of people never left their hometown, yet now she lives in a world where the vast majority of people can reach any place on the globe in less than twenty-four hours.

Think also of how entertainment has changed in Mildred Schappals's lifetime. She was two years old when the first radio sent out its first commercial broadcast. She was ten when WRGB became the first television station. She watched movies transition from black-and-white to full color to 3D to HD to IMAX to 4K Ultra and beyond. As a young woman, she had a handful of programming options to watch. Today, the amount of cable channels and streaming platforms and self-produced content feels almost infinite. Her choices are unlimited.

Explore the Scripture

My point is that our worldwide accumulation of information has increased at exponential levels during the past hundred years. We have more knowledge available at our fingertips now than at any point in human history, and that access is accelerating at an incredible rate. For these reasons, I believe we are witnessing the fulfillment of another key prophecy in the book of Daniel:

"But you, Daniel, shut up the words, and seal the book until the time of the end; many shall run to and fro, and knowledge shall increase."

(DANIEL 12:4)

How should we interpret the phrase, "many shall run to and fro"?

What are some of the biggest shifts in technology that have occurred during your lifetime?

How has your life benefitted or improved through greater access to information?

In recent years, which scientific advancements or breakthroughs have made you most excited? Why?

In recent years, which scientific advancements or breakthroughs have made you feel apprehensive or afraid? Why?

Using the following scale, to what degree do you trust national and world leaders to use scientific advancements responsibly and for the good of all people?

1	2	3	4	5	6	7	8	9	10
		(No Trust)						(High Trust)	

One of the biggest questions we must address as citizens of the modern world is whether unfettered access to information is always a good thing. In other words, *Is there such a thing as too much knowledge?* The Bible offers a cautionary tale on that theme in the story commonly referred to as the Tower of Babel:

> ¹ *Now the whole earth had one language and one speech.* ² *And it came to pass, as they journeyed from the east, that they found a plain in the land of Shinar, and they dwelt there.* ³ *Then they said to one another, "Come, let us make bricks and bake them thoroughly." They had brick for stone, and they had asphalt for mortar.* ⁴ *And they said, "Come, let us build ourselves a city, and a tower whose top is in the heavens; let us make a name for ourselves, lest we be scattered abroad over the face of the whole earth."*
>
> ⁵ *But the LORD came down to see the city and the tower which the sons of men had built.* ⁶ *And the LORD said, "Indeed the people are one and they all have one language, and this is what they begin to do; now nothing that they propose to do will be withheld from them.* ⁷ *Come, let Us go down and there confuse their language, that they may not understand one another's speech."* ⁸ *So the LORD scattered them abroad from there over the face of all the earth, and they ceased building the city.* ⁹ *Therefore its name is called Babel, because there the LORD confused the language of all the earth; and from there the LORD scattered them abroad over the face of all the earth.*

(GENESIS 11:1–9)

What are your first impressions of this story?

How does the Tower of Babel represent an increase in human knowledge?

How does this story serve as a warning to our modern culture?

Reflect on the Scripture

The literal translation of the prophecy found in Daniel 12:4 indicates that an *explosion of knowledge* will occur at the End of the Age. This will be something quite different from the steady and stable advance of learning that defined our world from the time of Abraham all the way to the time of Sir Isaac Newton. No, Daniel was describing an *unprecedented* eruption of information.

I believe we are experiencing that eruption today—in more ways than one. In the last three generations, we have put men on the moon, robotically explored the surface of Mars, and made major advances in the medical field. Tiny babies weighing less than one pound can survive outside the womb, and the unborn can undergo surgery while in their mother's womb. We can repair DNA and clone sheep, mice, and cattle. We also have the technology to clone humans—and before too long, I am sure that we will.

All this knowledge should be a good thing, and there's no doubt that it has improved many facets of our lives. Still, mankind is heading toward a day of reckoning. The undeniable truth is that all this knowledge has not produced the stable utopia that we hoped for and have so earnestly sought. Instead, we have produced a people who know more about rock stars than history. Our "enlightened" society seeks freedom, self-expression, and safe places, but it is enslaved by perversion, narcissism, addictions, and hedonism.

We tout the benefits of secular humanism and the worship of human intellect, yet our enlightened, religion-free society finds itself impotent in the face of growing crime. Why? Because knowledge without God can only produce intellectual barbarians. We have forgotten—or ignored—the apostle Paul's warnings about the wisdom of this world:

> [20] *Where is the wise? Where is the scribe? Where is the disputer of this age? Has not God made foolish the wisdom of this world?* [21] *For since, in the wisdom of God, the world through wisdom did not know God, it pleased God through the foolishness of the message preached to save those who believe.* [22] *For Jews request a sign, and Greeks seek after wisdom;* [23] *but we preach Christ crucified, to the Jews a stumbling block and to the Greeks foolishness,* [24] *but to those who are called, both Jews and Greeks, Christ the power of God and the wisdom of God.* [25] *Because the foolishness of God is wiser than men, and the weakness of God is stronger than men.*
>
> (1 CORINTHIANS 1:20–25)

To what was Paul referring when he described "the wisdom of this world"?

How would you define the wisdom of the world today? Make a list of some of the primary values and beliefs that form the core of modern culture.

In what ways does Scripture as a whole and the gospel in particular represent a form of "foolishness" to the world?

When have you experienced the "foolishness" of God to be wiser than human wisdom?

Act in Faith

As participants in the modern world, it's easy to be lulled into a false sense of security. We are not only more informed than any other generation in human history, but we are also *more* entertained. We are *more* comfortable . . . *more* self-indulged . . . and *more* distracted than generations before us. Yet, the *more* we get—the *more* we want.

Sadly, this is true even of many within the church. Many believers who claim to be citizens of God's kingdom are often indistinguishable from the citizens of this secular culture. But we must remember that these times of comfort and (false) security will not last. We must be aware that the period of increased knowledge prophesied by Daniel was only a step away from the End of the Age. When this season of prosperity comes to an end, the world as we know it will reach its tipping point and plunge headlong into the Great Tribulation.

We have built a society based on the pillars of technology, a capitalistic economy, and human government. Just like in the times of Babel, we have conveniently forgotten (or deliberately ignored) God's precepts and warnings in order to go our own way. But as the clock nears midnight, my friend, the birth pangs of the coming End of the Age are starting to send shock waves throughout civilization. The pillars of our society are teetering . . . and soon they will fall.

Our actions today will determine whether we are appropriately prepared for what is coming tomorrow.

Where do you see evidence in the world today that our systems and societies are not as stable as they seem?

What are some specific ways you can prepare for the coming End of the Age?

What are some ways that you can use this season of increased knowledge as a tool to help advance the kingdom of God?

Prayer is our path to the Throne; it is essential to our spiritual survival. Sometimes, "I'll pray about it" sounds trite or overly religious, but in truth, prayer offers us the chance to bring God's strength to bear rather than our own. It is the key to unlocking God's wisdom. Remember how Daniel responded when he became aware that the seventy years of exile for the Israelites were drawing to a close:

> [3] *Then I set my face toward the Lord God to make request by prayer and supplications, with fasting, sackcloth, and ashes.* [4] *And I prayed to the LORD my God, and made confession, and said, "O Lord, great and awesome God, who keeps His covenant and mercy with those who love Him, and with those who keep His commandments,* [5] *we have sinned and committed iniquity, we have done wickedly and rebelled, even by departing from Your precepts and Your judgments.* [6] *Neither have we heeded Your servants the prophets, who spoke in Your name to our kings and our princes, to our fathers and all the people of the land.* [7] *O Lord, righteousness belongs to You, but to us shame of face, as it is this day—to the men of Judah, to the inhabitants of Jerusalem and all Israel, those near and those far off in all the countries to which You have driven them, because of the unfaithfulness which they have committed against You.*

(DANIEL 9:3–7)

How can you pray for the leaders of your community and your local government in the weeks to come? What issues or opportunities are most pressing?

How can you pray for the leaders of your nation in the weeks to come? Where do you see opportunities for God's wisdom to flourish?

How can you pray for the leaders of the world in the weeks to come? What are some major problems that can only be solved through God's strength?

Responsive Prayer: *Heavenly Father, I confess that I have lived at times more as a member of this world than as a citizen of heaven. In the name of Jesus Christ, I repent of any choices I have made while attempting to keep one foot in Your kingdom and one foot in this world. By Your power, Lord God, and by the power of Your Spirit, I submit to Your wisdom, and I commit to doing whatever work is necessary for the advancement of Your kingdom. Amen.*

NOTE
1. Jade Scipioni, "Life Lessons from a 102-Year-Old who Survived Covid, the Spanish Flu and Two Types of Cancer," CNBC (August 11, 2020), https://www.cnbc.com/2020/08/11/lessons-from-102-year-old-who-survived-covid-flu-pandemic-cancer.html.

11:53 PM

The Great Escape

Then we who are alive and remain shall be caught up together with them in the clouds to meet the Lord in the air. And thus we shall always be with the Lord.

1 Thessalonians 4:17

Yes, my friend, the Son of God, Jesus Christ, will come for His Church at the Rapture. Those who have placed their faith in Him will be instantly transported into heaven.

From Chapter 4 of *The End of the Age*

Harold Camping was a pastor and ministry leader in California who made headlines, attracted followers—and also raised millions of dollars—by predicting the world would end on May 21, 2011. He spoke about this date and delivered his predictions with confidence, claiming they were revealed in the Bible.

Camping was also explosively public about his belief. He built a large radio network to broadcast his predictions over the airwaves. His ministry spent millions on billboards and advertisements around the world. He even implored his supporters to act with confidence in the coming end by divesting themselves of possessions and draining their bank accounts in anticipation of Judgment Day.

But Camping was wrong. May 21, 2011, came and went—and the world continued. Undeterred, Camping revised his prediction to October 21, 2011. Once again, he confidently asserted that his claims were rooted in Scripture. He directed his followers to rid themselves of earthly goods and worldly wealth in anticipation of the end. And once again, he was wrong. October 21, 2011, came and went. Camping passed away two years later at the age of 92 and the world moved on.

It's easy to laugh off these incidents as silly. Unfortunately, those same incidents make it easy for the world in general to laugh off the idea that judgment is coming. Remember, the Bible makes two definite declarations regarding the End of the Age. First, *there will be an end*. In the words of Jesus: "This gospel of the kingdom will be preached in all the world as a witness to all the nations, and then the end will come" (Matthew 24:14). Second, *no person will know or predict the day of that end*: "But of that day and hour no one knows, not even the angels of heaven, but My Father only" (verse 36).

Preachers like Harold Camping ignore that second truth about the End of the Age—and we rightly criticize them for it. However, in offering such criticism, we must not allow ourselves to ignore the first truth—that an end to this age *is coming*. The mystery that we call the Rapture will be the critical sign or confirmation that the End of the Age is at hand.

Explore the Scripture

The Good News of Christ's resurrection spread like wildfire throughout Asia Minor and many believers were being persecuted, even tortured to death, for their faith by religious extremists and political dictators. However, few experienced the level of pain and suffering that the Apostle Paul endured. He was beaten and left for dead. He was falsely accused and imprisoned. He endured shipwrecks, isolation, extreme hunger and thirst, and he became a regular object of scorn and hatred in the different regions where he preached the message of the gospel (see 2 Corinthians 11:24–28).

In the midst of all this turmoil, many early Christians began to wonder whether they were living in the end times. Were they enduring the persecutions and tribulations prophesied by Daniel? Paul answered them in his epistles with a word-picture of the Rapture. Here are two examples:

[51] *Behold, I tell you a mystery: We shall not all sleep, but we shall all be changed—* [52] *in a moment, in the twinkling of an eye, at the last trumpet. For the trumpet will sound, and the dead will be raised incorruptible, and we shall be changed.* [53] *For this corruptible must put on incorruption, and this mortal must put on immortality.* [54] *So when this corruptible has put on incorruption, and this mortal has put on immortality, then shall be brought to pass the saying that is written: "Death is swallowed up in victory."*

(1 CORINTHIANS 15:51–54)

[13] *But I do not want you to be ignorant, brethren, concerning those who have fallen asleep, lest you sorrow as others who have no hope.* [14] *For if we believe that Jesus died and rose again, even so God will bring with Him those who sleep in Jesus.*

[15] *For this we say to you by the word of the Lord, that we who are alive and remain until the coming of the Lord will by no means precede those who are asleep.* [16] *For the Lord Himself will descend from heaven with a shout, with the voice of an archangel, and with the trumpet of God. And the dead in Christ will rise first.* [17] *Then we who are alive and remain shall be caught up together with them in the clouds to meet the Lord in the air. And thus we shall always be with the Lord.* [18] *Therefore comfort one another with these words.*

(1 THESSALONIANS 4:13–18)

35

What are some words or phrases from those passages that catch your attention? Why?

How would you describe Paul's use of "sleep" and "asleep" in these passages?

How will the Rapture fulfill the saying, "Death is swallowed up in victory" (1 Corinthians 15:54)?

What is the connection between Jesus' resurrection and the Rapture?

What can we say for certain about the Rapture based on these passages? What do we know to be true?

How does the Rapture provide an opportunity for "comfort" (1 Thessalonians 4:18) among God's people?

It's important to remember that our understanding of the Rapture is not based only on prophecy. Instead, the reality of the Rapture is also connected to real-world events that have already taken place. By this, I mean moments from history that both prove God's power to enact the Rapture and point forward to the day when He will do so. Jesus' ascension into heaven is the most startling of these examples:

> [9] *Now when He had spoken these things, while they watched, He was taken up, and a cloud received Him out of their sight.* [10] *And while they looked steadfastly toward heaven as He went up, behold, two men stood by them in white apparel,* [11] *who also said, "Men of Galilee, why do you stand gazing up into heaven? This same Jesus, who was taken up from you into heaven, will so come in like manner as you saw Him go into heaven."*
>
> (ACTS 1:9–11)

How does this moment highlight God's ability to enact the Rapture?

What effect did Jesus' ascension have on those who witnessed it? On the early church?

How do the angels' words increase your understanding of what the Rapture will be and how it will be accomplished?

Reflect on the Scripture

Before we go any further in this lesson, let's get on the same page in terms of definitions. The *Rapture* is defined as an occurrence when the Church— all believers, living and dead—will be translated or resurrected into heaven. The Tribulation is the final "week" of the Seventy Weeks described in the book of Daniel.[1] It represents seven years in which God will punish the Gentile nations of the world for their rebellion, even as He prepares Israel for restoration and regeneration (see Deuteronomy 4:29-30; Jeremiah 30:4-11; Ezekiel 20:22-44; 22:13-22).

It is important to note that many Bible scholars and followers of Jesus hold different viewpoints on critical aspects of the Rapture and its connection to the Tribulation. For example, the "Partial Rapture" position says that when Jesus comes in the clouds of glory, He will take only those who have had a second work of grace or who are sanctified in their daily lives. According to this view, the body of Christ will be divided into two parts: (1) a sanctified part that will ascend into heaven, and (2) an unsanctified part that will be left to go through the Tribulation in the hope that their sins may be purged through this great time of trial.

This view must be rejected on the basis that the death of Jesus Christ removes all sin. As God states, "Their sins [those who repent] and their lawless deeds I will remember no more" (Hebrews 10:17). Because our redemption at Calvary was complete, God will receive everyone who has confessed Christ as Lord and accepted His substitutionary death at Calvary. Moreover, Paul affirms in 1 Corinthians 12:13 that the church is "one body."

Other differences pertain to when the Rapture will take place. The "Midtribulation Rapture" is the belief that the Church will endure the first three and one-half years of the Tribulation and then be raptured into heaven. Those who adopt a "Post-Tribulation Rapture" view believe that Christians will endure all seven years of the Tribulation before they are caught up in the air to meet with

Christ. And the "Pre-Wrath Rapture" approach states that the Church will experience five and one-half years of the Tribulation before being raptured.

It is my view that all of these positions are in error. Why? Because the best reading of prophetic Scripture teaches us that the collected body of Christians—what we call the Church—will not experience the suffering and intense persecution associated with the Tribulation. This viewpoint is called the "Pretribulation Rapture," and it best aligns with the teachings of God's Word for several reasons.

First, the very nature of the Tribulation precludes the Church from suffering any of it. The Tribulation is a horrendous time of wrath, judgment, indignation, darkness, destruction, and death—and it leads to the End of the Age. Yet Paul wrote, "There is therefore now no condemnation [judgment] to those who are in Christ Jesus" (Romans 8:1). The Church has been cleansed by the blood of Jesus and needs no other purification.

Second, I believe the Pre-Tribulation Rapture position is scripturally correct due to Paul's teaching in 2 Thessalonians 2. As mentioned earlier, many in the early church began to wonder if the intense persecution they were enduring in the ancient world was evidence of the Tribulation. Paul told them "not to be soon shaken in mind or troubled, either by spirit or by word or by letter, as if from us, as though the day of Christ [the Day of the Lord] had come" (verse 2).

Paul said they were not in the Tribulation. He wrote, "that Day will not come unless the falling away comes first, and the man of sin is revealed, the son of perdition" (verse 3). The "man of sin" is the coming Antichrist, who will come from the federated states of Europe, the final form of Gentile world power. He will be the leader of the "ten toes" that Daniel saw in his dream of the statue with the head of gold.

The Antichrist has not appeared yet, "for the mystery of lawlessness is already at work; only He who now restrains [hinders] will do so [keep on hindering] until He is taken out of the way" (verse 7). Who is restraining Satan from presenting the Antichrist to the world? The Holy Spirit, who indwells and empowers the Church. When the Church leaves the earth, the Holy Spirit will leave with it. Accordingly, when Jesus appears in the clouds of heaven to rapture the Church from the earth, God's restraint will be removed, and Satan can then accomplish his aim of dominating the world through the work of the Antichrist.

Third, Revelation 4:4 describes elders surrounding the throne of Christ that are clearly symbolic of the Church, which means those elders have been removed from earth prior to the Tribulation. And fourth, in 2 Thessalonians 1:7–8, Paul reminds his readers that the Tribulation is intended as a pouring out of wrath against "those who do not know God." That does not include the Church.

How would you summarize each of the five views on the Rapture?

- The Partial Rapture:

- The Midtribulation Rapture:

- The Post-Tribulation Rapture:

- The Pre-Wrath Rapture:

- The Pretribulation Rapture:

Why is it important for Christians to have an understanding of Rapture and how it will work?

What emotions do you experience when you contemplate the reality of God's judgment and the Tribulation?

What emotions do you experience when you contemplate the Rapture of the Church? Why?

In *The End of the Age,* I note that in order to understand the meaning behind some of the symbolic language used to describe the Rapture, we must understand some of the nuptial chain of events in a traditional Hebrew wedding:

> In the ancient biblical ceremony, the bridegroom or an agent of the bridegroom's father went out in search of a bride. . . . If it was a good match, a bride or her family would often agree to the marriage without ever seeing the future groom. Next, a price would be established for the bride. . . .
>
> Finally, the groom would present the bride with gifts. Most grooms today give their brides a ring as evidence of love and commitment, but in ancient times the gift could have been almost anything. If the bride accepted her groom's gift, they shared a cup of wine, called the cup of the covenant, and the betrothal was complete. Before leaving her home, the groom would tell his bride, "I go to prepare a place for you. I will return again to you.". . .
>
> This is a powerful word picture of what God has prepared for us! We are the betrothed bride of Christ, sought by the Holy Spirit and purchased at Calvary with the precious blood of Jesus. Paul said, "For you were bought at a price" (1 Corinthians 6:20). The Almighty Father looked down from heaven and accepted the price of our redemption. We, the bride, accepted the Groom and the evidence of His love for us. Our betrothal contract is the Word of God, for it contains every promise our loving Groom has made on our behalf. . . .
>
> As we wait for our Bridegroom, Jesus has returned to His Father's house to prepare everything for our arrival. Before He departed this earth, Jesus said, "In My Father's house are many mansions; if it were not so, I would have told you. I go to prepare a place for you. And if I go

and prepare a place for you, I will come again and receive you to Myself; that where I am, there you may be also" (John 14:2–3).[2]

How does this picture of a Jewish wedding enhance your understanding of the Rapture and what God is doing on your behalf?

Act in Faith

As Paul continued to teach the early Christians about the future reality of God's judgment and the End of the Age, he offered this important perspective: "For we must all appear before the judgment seat of Christ, that each one may receive the things done in the body, according to what he has done, whether good or bad" (2 Corinthians 5:10). This scene of judgment is often called the *bema seat* of Christ.

In ancient Greece, the bema seat was never used as a judicial bench where criminals were either pardoned or sentenced. Instead, it referred to a raised platform in the sports arena on which the umpire sat. From this platform, the judge rewarded all contestants and winners. As Christians, we run the race set before us. If we play by the rules established in the Word of God, we will be ushered to the bema seat to stand—not before heads of state, but before the Son of God. We shall not hear the words "guilty" or "innocent" in that place; rather, we shall receive the rewards of our good and faithful service.

Specifically, on display at the bema seat will be five great crowns bestowed upon the bride as the loyal and trustworthy servants of Christ. These are:

- **The crown of life.** Given to steadfast believers tested by prison and persecution even to the point of death (see Revelation 2:10).

- **The crown of glory.** A never-tarnishing crown given to the self-sacrificing pastor who shepherds his flock (see 1 Peter 5:2–4).

- **The crown of righteousness.** Everyone who runs life's race with patience, endurance, and perseverance will receive this crown (see 2 Timothy 4:8).

- **The crown of rejoicing.** Evangelists and soul winners can eagerly anticipate receiving this crown (see 1 Thessalonians 2:19–20).

- **The victor's crown.** Given to those who overcame all for the sake of the gospel (see 1 Corinthians 9:25).

Which of these crowns are you especially excited to receive? Why?

What motivates you to stay faithful in your spiritual walk each day?

The Rapture is a landmark that has been cemented in our future as followers of Jesus. How should that reality impact your decisions in the present?

What are some major decisions that are upcoming in your life? List three.

1.

2.

3.

What impact should the certainty of the Rapture have on those decisions?

Responsive Prayer: *Lord Jesus, I affirm the truth of Scripture that you ascended in heaven as an act of power and as a display of Your victory over death. I affirm the truth of Scripture that You will return in that same power to establish an even greater victory. By the power of Your blood that was shed on the cross, I commit to prepare myself for the reality of Your return. Amen.*

NOTES
1. Thomas D. Ice, "Why I Believe the Bible Teaches Rapture Before Tribulation," Scholars Crossing, Liberty University, May 2009, https://digitalcommons.liberty.edu/cgi/viewcontent.cgi?article=1117&context=pretrib_arch.
2. John Hagee, *The End of the Age*, pp. 121–124.

11:54 PM

Russia Invades Israel

Then you [Russia] will come from your place out of the far north, you and many peoples with you, all of them riding on horses, a great company and a mighty army. You will come up against My people Israel like a cloud, to cover the land. It will be in the latter days that I will bring you against My land, so that the nations may know Me, when I am hallowed in you.

Ezekiel 38:15–16

Make no mistake—at some moment in the countdown to the End of the Age . . . Russia, together with Iran, Turkey, Libya, and the radical Islamic Arab nations, will lead a massive attack upon the nation of Israel.

From Chapter 5 of *The End of the Age*

Do you remember the Russian invasion of Crimea back in 2014?
The systematic takeover, planned and initiated by Vladimir Putin, was a huge event in terms of global politics, yet it largely went under the radar at the time. Today, it seems almost forgotten by most people outside of the regions directly involved. As one writer described it, "The annexation of Crimea was the smoothest invasion of modern times. It was over before the outside world realized it had even started."[1]

The invasion began in January 2014 when Putin quietly started sending in thousands of extra troops to "protect" Russian military bases inside the Crimean peninsula, which at the time was the southern tip of Ukraine. Other volunteers living within Crimea joined the soldiers and, in a coordinated movement, by March had sealed off all the entry and exit points to that peninsula. Before the international community even had time to process what had happened, Crimea changed from the southern tip of Ukraine to the western spur of Russia.

Other nations erupted in protest once it became clear what had occurred. Some leaders of the international community offered strong words—and a few even backed up those words with sanctions. Yet, in the end, none of it mattered. Putin's brazen theft was complete.

In more recent years, Russia has regularly made headlines by sticking its collective nose where it did not belong—from attempting to influence elections, to supporting (or actively engaging) cyber criminals, to funding terrorists and strongman regimes in Syria and other nations throughout the Middle East. Again and again, Putin and Russia have displayed their willingness to ruffle feathers and flaunt international law to further the Russian agenda.

Today, Russia continues to be a dominant force in Europe and the surrounding regions, desperate to achieve the former glory and influence it enjoyed during the Cold War as the U.S.S.R. There is no doubt that Russia possesses the will and the cunning to accomplish its ends. Furthermore, as we will see in this lesson, one of those ends will include Russia turning its attention and malice toward the nation of Israel.

Explore the Scripture

There is a great deal of evidence to support the claim that Russia will lead a coalition against Israel in the near future—an attack that will fulfill the prophecy of Ezekiel 38–39, which we will explore below. But first, let's review some background information about the nation.

Since the turn of the century, Vladimir Putin has taken several steps to increase Russian influence in the Middle East. For example, Russia has negotiated arms deals in Syria worth billions of dollars. Russia has signed military treaties with Turkey and trade agreements with the United Arab Emirates. Perhaps most sinister of all, Russia is a key sponsor (along with Iran) of Hezbollah, which is a highly trained and sophisticated terrorist group in Lebanon whose primary aim is the complete destruction of Israel.

How does Israel factor in with Russia's plans? Putin has his eye on Israel due to its strategic geographical position, its large natural-gas deposits, and its warm-water seaports. When you add these factors together, it's only logical to believe that Russia is the leader of the future attack against Israel. Scripture describes this coming conflict in the book of Ezekiel:

[1] Now the word of the LORD came to me, saying, [2] "Son of man, set your face against Gog, of the land of Magog, the prince of Rosh, Meshech, and Tubal, and prophesy against him, [3] and say, 'Thus says the Lord GOD: "Behold, I am against you, O Gog, the prince of Rosh, Meshech, and Tubal. [4] I will turn you around, put hooks into your jaws, and lead you out, with all your army, horses, and horsemen, all splendidly clothed, a great company with bucklers and shields, all of them handling swords. [5] Persia, Ethiopia, and Libya are with them, all of them with shield and helmet; [6] Gomer and all its troops; the house of Togarmah from the far north and all its troops—many people are with you. . . .

[10] 'Thus says the Lord GOD: "On that day it shall come to pass that thoughts will arise in your mind, and you will make an evil plan: [11] You will say, 'I will go up against a land of unwalled villages; I will go to a peaceful people, who dwell safely, all of them dwelling without walls, and having neither bars nor gates'— [12] to take plunder and to take booty, to stretch out your hand against the waste places that are again inhabited, and against a people gathered from the nations, who have acquired livestock and goods, who dwell in the midst of the land. [13] Sheba, Dedan, the merchants of Tarshish, and all their young lions will say to you, 'Have you come to take plunder? Have you gathered your army to take booty, to carry away silver and gold, to take away livestock and goods, to take great plunder?' " '

¹⁴ *"Therefore, son of man, prophesy and say to Gog, 'Thus says the Lord GOD: "On that day when My people Israel dwell safely, will you not know it?* ¹⁵ *Then you will come from your place out of the far north, you and many peoples with you, all of them riding on horses, a great company and a mighty army.* ¹⁶ *You will come up against My people Israel like a cloud, to cover the land. It will be in the latter days that I will bring you against My land, so that the nations may know Me, when I am hallowed in you, O Gog, before their eyes."* ¹⁷ *Thus says the Lord GOD: "Are you he of whom I have spoken in former days by My servants the prophets of Israel, who prophesied for years in those days that I would bring you against them?*

(EZEKIEL 38:1–6, 10–17)

What stands out as most interesting or important from these verses? Why?

How would you describe the tone of God's words in this prophecy?

How should we understand the language of *horses*, *horsemen*, *shields*, and *swords*, given that these prophecies are referencing events still to come?

God identified the invaders that will join Russia as Persia, Ethiopia, Libya, Gomer, and Togarmah (see verses 5–6). Persia is Iran. Ethiopia and Libya refer to the Arab Islamic nations of the Arabian Peninsula. Gomer and Togarmah most likely refer to the region now occupied by the nation of Turkey. According to verses 10 and following, what are the primary goals of this coalition that will align against Israel?

What might be some modern motivations for nations such as Russia, Iran, Turkey, and the Arab states to attack or invade Israel?

What about the results of this surprise attack? Does Scripture give us a hint as to whether Russia and its allies will succeed? It gives us more than a hint, actually—the Bible paints a clear and detailed picture of Israel's victory.

God said that when Gog sweeps down from the north, "My fury will show in My face" (Ezekiel 38:18). The Lord—having watched the Jews of the Holocaust walk into the gas chambers, after seeing the "apple of His eye" thrown into the ovens and their ashes dumped by the tons into the rivers of Europe, after seeing the "land of milk and honey" run red with Jewish blood in five major wars for peace and freedom—will stand up and shout to the nations of the world. He will shatter His silence and say, "Enough!" We read about the result:

[18] *"And it will come to pass at the same time, when Gog comes against the land of Israel," says the Lord God, "that My fury will show in My face.* [19] *For in My jealousy and in the fire of My wrath I have spoken: 'Surely in that day there shall be a great earthquake in the land of Israel,* [20] *so that the fish of the sea, the birds of the heavens, the beasts of the field, all creeping things that creep on the earth, and all*

men who are on the face of the earth shall shake at My presence. The mountains shall be thrown down, the steep places shall fall, and every wall shall fall to the ground.' ²¹ I will call for a sword against Gog throughout all My mountains," says the Lord GOD. "Every man's sword will be against his brother. ²² And I will bring him to judgment with pestilence and bloodshed; I will rain down on him, on his troops, and on the many peoples who are with him, flooding rain, great hailstones, fire, and brimstone. ²³ Thus I will magnify Myself and sanctify Myself, and I will be known in the eyes of many nations. Then they shall know that I am the LORD."

(EZEKIEL 38:18–23)

How would you summarize the events described in this passage? What will happen during this conflict between Russia and Israel?

What are the key images mentioned in these verses? What do they convey?

Which characteristics of God are emphasized in these verses?

What is God's motivation or purpose during this conflict?

Reflect on the Scripture

There are two elements of this prophecy in Ezekiel 38–39 that are especially interesting. The first is the way in which these events both illustrate and highlight God's sovereignty. Look again at Ezekiel 38:4, in which God is speaking to Rosh (Russia): "I will turn you around, put hooks into your jaws, and lead you out, with all your army, horses, and horsemen, all splendidly clothed, a great company *with* bucklers and shields, all of them handling swords."

In the theatre of your mind, imagine the vast army of Russia and its allies, all arrayed in military splendor. Men and women with grim faces and cold eyes, their weapons all shining in the sun. See the colorful panorama of uniforms as several nations, armies, and battalions march together as one. Envision the power of thousands of vehicles of war—lined up, tuned up, and selecting targets with drone-assisted precision.

This is a mighty scene! And yet who is in charge of it all? Not Vladimir Putin or any other world leader. Not generals or even religious extremists. *God* is sovereign! He is the One who has "put hooks into [their] jaws," leading them out like fish on a line, helpless and defenseless.

How would you define God's sovereignty and what does it mean to you?

How does God's sovereignty affect our lives, our nation and the world?

Can God's sovereignty (Divine Authority) and our personal will co-exist? Why or why not?

Where do you see evidence of God's sovereignty in history?

Where do you see evidence of God's sovereignty at work today?

A second interesting truth is that Russia's failed attack against Israel will be one of the sparks that rekindles Israel's connection to God. The Lord's display of power in the victory over Russia and her allies will testify to His beloved Jewish people that He alone is their God. Through their miraculous deliverance, the hearts of the Jewish people will begin to turn again to the God of Abraham, Isaac, and Jacob:

> [22] *So the house of Israel shall know that I am the* Lord *their God from that day forward.* [23] *The Gentiles shall know that the house of Israel went into captivity for their iniquity; because they were unfaithful to Me, therefore I hid My face from them. I gave them into the hand of their enemies, and they all fell by the sword.* [24]

According to their uncleanness and according to their transgressions I have dealt with them, and hidden My face from them." '

25 "Therefore thus says the Lord GOD: 'Now I will bring back the captives of Jacob, and have mercy on the whole house of Israel; and I will be jealous for My holy name— 26 after they have borne their shame, and all their unfaithfulness in which they were unfaithful to Me, when they dwelt safely in their own land and no one made them afraid. 27 When I have brought them back from the peoples and gathered them out of their enemies' lands, and I am hallowed in them in the sight of many nations, 28 then they shall know that I am the LORD their God, who sent them into captivity among the nations, but also brought them back to their land, and left none of them captive any longer. 29 And I will not hide My face from them anymore; for I shall have poured out My Spirit on the house of Israel,' says the Lord GOD."

(EZEKIEL 39:22–29)

How should we understand the word *know* in these verses?

When has God used difficult circumstances to catch your attention or deepen your relationship with Him?

Act in Faith

Why will God allow the nations to make war upon Israel? There is only one answer: for His glory. Ezekiel wrote, "I will magnify Myself and sanctify Myself, and I will be known in the eyes of many nations. Then they shall know that I am the LORD. . . . So the house of Israel shall know that I am the LORD their God from that day forward" (Ezekiel 38:23; 39:22).

Mankind worships a pantheon of so-called gods. Some worship Buddha, others Muhammad, some Satan, and some worship gods of their own making, but who is the Almighty God? When the God of Abraham, Isaac, and Jacob destroys the enemies of Israel, there will be no doubt that He is the One and only Jehovah God: "It will be in the latter days that I will bring you against My land, so that the nations may know Me, when I am hallowed in you, O Gog, before their eyes" (Ezekiel 38:16).

Truly, the only way we will be able to understand the significance of this incredible defeat is to accept it as an act of God. Ezekiel wanted the world to know that God will supernaturally neutralize the enemies of Israel so that His Name might be glorified. Yet we don't have to wait for these events to unfold in order to find opportunities to glorify our great God and Eternal Savior. We have that privilege every day. Including today! Let that reality be your focus as we conclude this lesson. Read aloud the following psalm as an act of praise to God:

> ¹ *Praise the LORD!*
>
> *Praise the LORD from the heavens;*
> *Praise Him in the heights!*
> ² *Praise Him, all His angels;*
> *Praise Him, all His hosts!*
> ³ *Praise Him, sun and moon;*
> *Praise Him, all you stars of light!*
> ⁴ *Praise Him, you heavens of heavens,*
> *And you waters above the heavens!*
>
> ⁵ *Let them praise the name of the LORD,*
> *For He commanded and they were created.*
> ⁶ *He also established them forever and ever;*
> *He made a decree which shall not pass away.*

*⁷ Praise the L*ORD *from the earth,*
   You great sea creatures and all the depths;
⁸ Fire and hail, snow and clouds;
   Stormy wind, fulfilling His word;
⁹ Mountains and all hills;
   Fruitful trees and all cedars;
¹⁰ Beasts and all cattle;
   Creeping things and flying fowl;
¹¹ Kings of the earth and all peoples;
   Princes and all judges of the earth;
¹² Both young men and maidens;
   Old men and children.

*¹³ Let them praise the name of the L*ORD,
   For His name alone is exalted;
   His glory is above the earth and heaven.
¹⁴ And He has exalted the horn of His people,
   The praise of all His saints—
   Of the children of Israel,
   A people near to Him.

   *Praise the L*ORD!

(PSALM 148:1–14)

What does it look like for you to glorify God in your everyday life?

What are some specific opportunities you will have this week to praise God and point others toward His goodness?

What are some specific circumstances you are experiencing right now that allow you to demonstrate trust in God's sovereignty?

Responsive Prayer: *Lord God, I affirm the truth of Your Word that You never slumber nor sleep. No matter what I experience or what I endure, You are with me. You are in control of all my circumstances. I praise You, Heavenly Father. I worship You. To the best of my ability, I commit to reflecting and uplifting Your glory throughout this week. Amen.*

Note

1. John Simpson, "Russia's Crimea Plan Detailed, Secret and Successful," BBC (March 19, 2014), https://www.bbc.com/news/world-europe-26644082.

11:55 PM

The Time of the Tribulation Begins

See that you are not troubled; for all these things must come to pass, but the end is not yet. For nation will rise against nation, and kingdom against kingdom. And there will be famines, pestilences, and earthquakes in various places. All these are the beginning of sorrows.

Matthew 24:6–8

The word Tribulation *strikes terror into the hearts of men, and justly so. God's portrait of the seven-year Tribulation reveals a time of unspeakable horror that can only be described as hell on earth. . . . God Almighty will pour out His awesome power on the whole world.*

From Chapter 6 of *The End of the Age*

Throughout human history, vast numbers of people and major regions of the globe have been ruled by dominating personalities. Just consider a few of the power players who have literally shaped the course of humanity:

- **Ramses II** (1303–1213 BCE): The most powerful pharaoh of Egypt's New Kingdom who led military expeditions into Canaan and Nubia and built cities, temples, and monuments. Known as the "Ruler of rulers." Ramses II oppressed the Jewish people while they were in Egyptian exile.

- **Nebuchadnezzar II** (642–562 BCE): The Babylonian empire's greatest king who is famous for his military campaigns, his construction projects, and the role he played in the Diaspora and enslavement of the Jewish people after he conquered Jerusalem .

- **Xerxes I** (518–465 BCE): King of the Persian empire (modern day Iran) reigned over 127 provinces spread across three million square miles and is featured in the book of Esther.

- **Alexander the Great** (356–323 BCE): King of the Greek kingdom of Macedon who conquered the vast Persian empire.

- **Augustus Caesar** (63 BCE–14 CE): First emperor of Rome, who reigned during the time of Christ, and allowed himself to be worshiped as a living god.

- **Charlemagne** (748–814 CE): King of the Franks who united the majority of western and central Europe during his rule by executing thousands of Saxons and members of various Germanic tribes who refused to convert to Christianity.

- **Genghis Khan** (1158–1227 CE): Warlord who united the nomadic tribes of northeast Asia and founded the Mongol Empire, which became the largest contiguous empire in history. He was responsible for the death of over 40 million people during his reign of terror.

- **Napoleon Bonaparte** (1769–1821 CE): Political and military leader of France who rose to power after the French Revolution. His brutality was considered the "blueprint" for Hitler. Napoleon used gas to exterminate the civil population of the Antilles, he created concentration camps in Corsica and Alba, and he re-established the slave trade, provoking the deaths of over 200,000 Africans in the French colonies.

- **Adolph Hitler** (1889–1945 CE): German dictator who invaded and annexed territories in Europe leading to World War II, and controlled areas of North Africa, Egypt, Libya, and Tunisia. Hitler perpetrated the Final Solution in which six million Jews and millions of other victims were systematically exterminated.

Each of these rulers exerted immense power. They viciously conquered their enemies and established kingdoms. These despots not only defined their own culture but also impacted future generations—for good or for evil. Yet the atrocities that will be committed by the ruler who is to come will make the past barbaric acts of these men seem like a walk in the park. And he will be known as the Antichrist.

The term *Antichrist* has become part of the jargon of our modern culture. For many, the concept of the Antichrist is connected to someone who is both evil and powerful—a supervillain out of a comic book. For others, the Antichrist is a label they throw at anyone they don't agree with. "Could this politician or that Big Tech executive be the Antichrist?"

However, as we'll see in this lesson, what Scripture reveals about the Antichrist is far removed from such pettiness and speculation. The Antichrist is real, and his impact on the world will be as massive as it will be terrifying. He will seize power after the Rapture of the Church and use that power to usher in a time of chaos and horror unlike anything the world has ever experienced: the Tribulation.

Explore the Scripture

As a reminder, we are currently living in a period where God has paused His prophetic clock. The death and resurrection of Jesus Christ occurred at the end of the sixty-ninth "week" as described in the prophetic vision of Daniel 9. The seventieth week will bring about the End of the Age (see 9:20–27).

But for now, we are in a time of waiting. God has placed Israel on a "sidetrack" so to say, in order to allow the Church to flourish. God's people have been accomplishing His work with varying degrees of success over the past 2,000 years. God's kingdom has advanced, and the gospel has been spread to the nations. Yet at the moment of the Rapture, when God instantly translates Christians from earth to heaven, the prophetic clock will start once more. With the Church gone, the world will enter into the seventieth week known as the Tribulation.

As we saw in the previous lesson, a Russian-led coalition will attempt to conquer Israel but be thwarted through God's miraculous provision and supernatural power. In the midst of that chaos, the Antichrist will ascend to the top of the world stage. We can read about this important figure in two key prophecies found in the book of Daniel:

23 *"And in the latter time of their kingdom,*
When the transgressors have reached their fullness,
A king shall arise,
Having fierce features,
Who understands sinister schemes.
24 *His power shall be mighty, but not by his own power;*
He shall destroy fearfully,
And shall prosper and thrive;
He shall destroy the mighty, and also the holy people.

25 *"Through his cunning*
He shall cause deceit to prosper under his rule;
And he shall exalt himself in his heart.
He shall destroy many in their prosperity.
He shall even rise against the Prince of princes;
But he shall be broken without human means.

26 *"And the vision of the evenings and mornings*
Which was told is true;
Therefore seal up the vision,
For it refers to many days in the future."

(DANIEL 8:23–26)

³⁶ *"Then the king shall do according to his own will: he shall exalt and magnify himself above every god, shall speak blasphemies against the God of gods, and shall prosper till the wrath has been accomplished; for what has been determined shall be done. ³⁷ He shall regard neither the God of his fathers nor the desire of women, nor regard any god; for he shall exalt himself above them all. ³⁸ But in their place he shall honor a god of fortresses; and a god which his fathers did not know he shall honor with gold and silver, with precious stones and pleasant things. ³⁹ Thus he shall act against the strongest fortresses with a foreign god, which he shall acknowledge, and advance its glory; and he shall cause them to rule over many, and divide the land for gain.*

(DANIEL 11:36–39)

What can you say for certain about the Antichrist based on these passages?

What are some personal characteristics or traits that will describe this man?

Where do you see evidence from these passages that the Antichrist is more than a regular human leader?

Based on these visions, what can we learn about the condition of the world during the time of the Antichrist's rise to power?

As we've seen, the Antichrist will not be an idle ruler. He will swiftly and ruthlessly bend the world to his will, and he will lead the global population into the eschatological period known as the Tribulation. Here again, many people today are familiar with that term—even those who do not follow Christ. Yet there is a great deal of confusion when it comes to *what* the Tribulation will be and *why* God will allow humanity to endure such a season of suffering.

Let's start with the *why*. The Bible gives us at least three reasons for the Tribulation:

1. To prepare for Israel's regeneration and restoration, bringing the nation into complete submission to the God of Abraham, Isaac, and Jacob in anticipation for the coming Messiah (see Jeremiah 30:11; Zechariah 12:10).

2. To punish the godless Gentile nations and all unbelievers for their sin of rejecting His Son, and for bowing before the Antichrist (see Revelation 16:2).

3. To demonstrate God's ultimate power in crushing the wicked nations of the world—especially those that have come against Israel.

In terms of the *what*, the Tribulation is a period of seven years in which God Almighty will pour out His awesome power on the whole world. There will be twenty-one separate acts of judgment on the earth associated with the Seven Seals, the Seven Trumpets, and the Seven Bowls (see Revelation 1–6; 8–9; 11; 16). Here is the apostle John's description of the events that will occur with the breaking of the Seven Seals:

[1] *Now I saw when the Lamb opened one of the seals; and I heard one of the four living creatures saying with a voice like thunder, "Come and see." [2] And I looked,*

and behold, a white horse. He who sat on it had a bow; and a crown was given to him, and he went out conquering and to conquer.

³ When He opened the second seal, I heard the second living creature saying, "Come and see." ⁴ Another horse, fiery red, went out. And it was granted to the one who sat on it to take peace from the earth, and that people should kill one another; and there was given to him a great sword.

⁵ When He opened the third seal, I heard the third living creature say, "Come and see." So I looked, and behold, a black horse, and he who sat on it had a pair of scales in his hand. ⁶ And I heard a voice in the midst of the four living creatures saying, "A quart of wheat for a denarius, and three quarts of barley for a denarius; and do not harm the oil and the wine."

⁷ When He opened the fourth seal, I heard the voice of the fourth living creature saying, "Come and see." ⁸ So I looked, and behold, a pale horse. And the name of him who sat on it was Death, and Hades followed with him. And power was given to them over a fourth of the earth, to kill with sword, with hunger, with death, and by the beasts of the earth.

⁹ When He opened the fifth seal, I saw under the altar the souls of those who had been slain for the word of God and for the testimony which they held. ¹⁰ And they cried with a loud voice, saying, "How long, O Lord, holy and true, until You judge and avenge our blood on those who dwell on the earth?" ¹¹ Then a white robe was given to each of them; and it was said to them that they should rest a little while longer, until both the number of their fellow servants and their brethren, who would be killed as they were, was completed.

¹² I looked when He opened the sixth seal, and behold, there was a great earthquake; and the sun became black as sackcloth of hair, and the moon became like blood. ¹³ And the stars of heaven fell to the earth, as a fig tree drops its late figs when it is shaken by a mighty wind. ¹⁴ Then the sky receded as a scroll when it is rolled up, and every mountain and island was moved out of its place. ¹⁵ And the kings of the earth, the great men, the rich men, the commanders, the mighty men, every slave and every free man, hid themselves in the caves and in the rocks of the mountains, ¹⁶ and said to the mountains and rocks, "Fall on us and hide us from the face of Him who sits on the throne and from the wrath of the Lamb! ¹⁷ For the great day of His wrath has come, and who is able to stand?"

(REVELATION 6:1–17)

THE END OF THE AGE STUDY GUIDE

In your own words, how would you describe the judgment unleashed by each of the first six seals?

- The first seal (verses 1–2):

- The second seal (verses 3–4):

- The third seal (verses 5–6):

- The fourth seal (verses 7–8):

- The fifth seal (verses 9–11):

- The sixth seal (verses 12–17):

The apostle John describes the Antichrist in Revelation 6:1–2. How does this description connect with what you read in Daniel 8:23–16 and 11:36–39?

Which images or descriptions especially capture your attention in Revelation 6:1–17? Why?

How does this passage reflect God's judgment and wrath?

How do these verses reflect God's justice? His love?

Reflect on the Scripture

The Antichrist will make his debut upon the stage of world history with hypnotic charm and charisma. As John writes, "Then I stood on the sand of the sea. And I saw a beast rising up out of the sea, having seven heads and ten horns, and on his horns ten crowns, and on his heads a blasphemous name" (Revelation 13:1).

Notice that the beast rose from the *sea*—which, in prophetic symbolism, represents the Gentile nations of the world. He will come from a confederation that was once part of the Roman Empire. At one point in history, the Roman Empire stretched from Ireland across to Germany, Switzerland, down to Egypt, and included Turkey, Iran, and Iraq. In Daniel's vision of the four beasts, the fourth beast had ten horns, which represented ten kingdoms (see Daniel 7:19–25). The little horn (the Antichrist), sprouted from among the other ten, which is believed to be the ten divisions of the old Roman Empire.

In his rise to power, the Antichrist will first weave his hypnotic spell over one nation in the ten-kingdom federation, and then over all ten. He will conquer three of the ten nations (the seven heads and ten crowns of Revelation 13:1), and then he will assume dominance over all of them. The Bible states that after the Antichrist's position is secure in the ten-nation federation, he will turn his predatory destruction toward the apple of God's eye—Israel.

The Antichrist's structure for world dominance will be built on three foundations:

1. **A one-world economy.** No longer will separate nations use separate currencies. Instead, the Tribulation will see a global economy built on a single, universal standard. More sinister, this economy will likely be all digital. Meaning, the Antichrist and his ruling class will have instant access to the financial and purchasing records of all people. Importantly, those who attempt to go "off the grid" and avoid this system will be prohibited from any kind of buying or selling. They and their families will be cut off.

2. **A one-world government.** Daniel prophesied the Antichrist will "devour the whole earth" (7:23) through the establishment of a single governing system. In this way, the Antichrist will complete the goal that Satan has been striving to achieve since Nimrod and the Tower of Babel: establishing a global power base through which he will attempt to challenge God Himself.

3. **A one-world religion.** More than any other descriptor, the Antichrist is a false version of Jesus the Savior. This demonic despot will be empowered by Satan rather than the Holy Spirit, and he will demand the worship that Satan has coveted since his expulsion from heaven. No other religious systems will be tolerated. All must worship the Antichrist and Satan.

As you look at today's world, where do you see evidence that a strong-man could seize power the way Scripture describes?

Where do you see the beginnings or foreshadowings of the Antichrist's three-pronged foundation?

- A one-world economy:

- A one-world government:

- A one-world religion:

How have recent advances in technology opened the door for those systems?

The chart below provides a brief description of the Seven Seals. Look up each of the corresponding passages and write down a description of the events in your own words. (For more information, refer to the section titled "The Seven Seals of the Tribulation" in chapter 6 of *The End of the Age*.)

Seal	Description
First Seal: *The Rider on the White Horse (Revelation 6:1–2)*	
Second Seal: *The Rider on the Red Horse (Revelation 6:3–4)*	

Seal	Description
Third Seal: *The Rider on the Black Horse (Revelation 6:5–6)*	
Fourth Seal: *The Rider on a Pale Horse (Revelation 6:7–8)*	
Fifth Seal: *The Martyrs (Revelation 6:9–11)*	
Sixth Seal: *Nature Revolts (Revelation 6:12–17)*	
Seventh Seal: *Silence in Heaven (Revelation 8:1)*	

How would you describe or explain the purpose behind these events? Why is it necessary for God to judge the world and pour out His wrath?

Act in Faith

The Tribulation will be a time of terror and anarchy that brings humanity to its knees. Even so, the grace of God will be on display through the continued outworking of His plan of salvation. People will come to Christ during the Tribulation who did not hear the gospel during the Dispensation of Grace. They will hear the gospel preached by angels flying through the heavens saying, "Fear God and give glory to Him, for the hour of His judgment has come; and worship Him who made heaven and earth" (Revelation 14:7). They will refuse to take the mark of the Antichrist, and they will be killed as martyrs.

Perhaps the Antichrist will charge them with treason. Perhaps he will condemn them for following what he might call "a dead religion for dead people." In any case, these martyrs will die for their faith, and their souls will wait in heaven until the Lord's purpose is complete.

We can be thankful that any friends or loved ones who are left behind and are forced to endure the Tribulation will not be instantly consigned to the eternal horrors of hell. They will have an opportunity to see the truth; see the Antichrist for who he is, and repent of their sins. Yet it should be our most fervent hope that all people hear the good news of the gospel on this side of the Rapture! In fact, it should be our fervent hope for *all* people—to share in God's desire that as many souls as possible may be spared from the terrible events of that final prophetic week.

I trust you feel this way. For that reason, I encourage you to participate in Jesus' saving work, by sharing the good news of the Gospel—so that the lost that come into your life will be spared the horrors of the Tribulation. Read Paul's words:

> [14] *How then shall they call on Him in whom they have not believed? And how shall they believe in Him of whom they have not heard? And how shall they hear without a preacher?* [15] *And how shall they preach unless they are sent? As it is written: "How beautiful are the feet of those who preach the gospel of peace, Who bring glad tidings of good things!"*
>
> (ROMANS 10:14–15)

Do you feel satisfied with your current efforts to share the gospel with those closest to you? Explain.

What steps can you take to be more assertive in bringing "glad tidings of good things"?

Who among your friends and family is in danger of experiencing the terrors of the Tribulation?

What step can you take this week to share the gospel with someone on that list?

Responsive Prayer: *Lord Jesus, I affirm the truth of Scripture that You "desire all men to be saved and to come to the knowledge of the truth." May Your Spirit fill my eyes so that I am able to see opportunities to preach the gospel. May Your Spirit fill my mouth with the right words to say. May Your Spirit fill my heart with love and courage to speak. And may You be glorified in those who accept Your free gift of salvation. Amen.*

11:56 PM

For Then Shall Come Great Tribulation

The first angel sounded: And hail and fire followed, mingled with blood, and they were thrown to the earth. And a third of the trees were burned up, and all green grass was burned up.

Revelation 8:7

The first time He came to earth, Jesus was the Lamb of God, led in silence to the slaughter— a death He willingly endured for our redemption. The next time He comes, He will be the Lion of the tribe of Judah who will trample His enemies until their blood stains His garments, and He shall rule with a rod of iron.

From Chapter 7 of *The End of the Age*

What comes to mind when you think about the book of Revelation? What images? What thoughts? What themes?

Many believe that the book of Revelation is primarily concerned with the future apocalypse, Armageddon, or the end of the world as we know it. They envision vivid imagery of the moon turning to blood, fire and brimstone, wormwood, and locusts with the stings of scorpions scouring the earth to torment all of mankind. Others connect Revelation with the political and economic ploys that will overshadow the world in years to come. This includes the Antichrist and his quest for global domination, along with the one-world government, one-world economy, and one-world religion we explored in the previous lesson.

Others—perhaps the more optimistic among us—primarily think about heaven when they ponder the book of Revelation. They think on images of God seated on His throne and Christ establishing His millennial kingdom. They picture the New Jerusalem with its glorious gates, healing waters, and throngs of worshipers from every tongue, tribe, and nation.

Let me be clear: each of these views and more, are present in the book of Revelation and play an important role within John's vision of God's revealed plan for the next phase of human history. Yet none are the primary focus of Revelation nor should they be our main focus as we read, study, and interpret this critically important book.

Instead, the Holy Spirit worked through the apostle John to reveal the primary purpose of the vision in the very first verse: "The Revelation of Jesus Christ, which God gave Him to show His servants—things which must shortly take place" (Revelation 1:1). The purpose of John's vision was to reveal the glory, wisdom, power, and the ultimate rule of the Son of God.

Explore the Scripture

So far in this study, we have focused primarily on the visions and writings of Daniel, the Jewish prophet living in Babylon between the fifth and sixth century BCE. As we've seen, the book of Daniel presents a critical framework and timeline for human history, both for our past and our future.

But now we will turn our attention more to John the Revelator—the man whom God's Spirit chose as the scribe for the book of Revelation. This is the same John who dropped his fishing nets by the shores of Galilee to follow a radical rabbi named Jesus of Nazareth. It is the same John who was in Christ's inner circle, along with Peter and James, and who was commissioned by the Lord to care for His mother as He hung on the cross. It is the same John who played a pivotal role in the early Church at Jerusalem after Christ's death and resurrection and who encouraged the churches of Asia with the triumphant message of their Redeemer. This is the John who wrote the fourth Gospel and also three epistles within the New Testament.

John was a beloved disciple and friend of Jesus who knew the voice of his Lord. So it only seems fitting that God chose him to help pull back the veil of history and reveal the End of the Age. At the time, John had been exiled to a small penal colony on the Isle of Patmos because of his testimony of Jesus Christ. According to the early church father Tertullian, John had been sent there by the Roman authorities in an attempt to silence him. The plan didn't work, for it was there that he recorded the vision known today as the book of Revelation.

John did not record the events of the End of the Age in strict chronological order. Revelation 6 through 18 deal with the Tribulation period, but chapters 12 and 13 take a sidetrack to supply brief biographical sketches of several key characters who also have prominent roles in Daniel's Seventieth Week account. And remember—while God's judgment is being poured out through the Seven Trumpets and Seven Vials, the Antichrist will continue to implement his scheme of world domination.

To better understand this time, we must see these events from both an earthly viewpoint and a heavenly one. To begin, here is a portion of John's vision that highlights the Antichrist, whom we first encountered in lesson 6:

[1] *Then I stood on the sand of the sea. And I saw a beast rising up out of the sea, having seven heads and ten horns, and on his horns ten crowns, and on his heads a blasphemous name.* [2] *Now the beast which I saw was like a leopard, his feet were like the feet of a bear, and his mouth like the mouth of a lion. The dragon gave him his power, his throne, and great authority.* [3] *And I saw one of his heads as if it had been mortally wounded, and his deadly wound was healed. And all the world marveled and followed the beast.* [4] *So they worshiped the dragon who gave authority to the beast; and they worshiped the beast, saying, "Who is like the beast? Who is able to make war with him?"*

⁵ And he was given a mouth speaking great things and blasphemies, and he was given authority to continue for forty-two months. ⁶ Then he opened his mouth in blasphemy against God, to blaspheme His name, His tabernacle, and those who dwell in heaven. ⁷ It was granted to him to make war with the saints and to overcome them. And authority was given him over every tribe, tongue, and nation. ⁸ All who dwell on the earth will worship him, whose names have not been written in the Book of Life of the Lamb slain from the foundation of the world.

⁹ If anyone has an ear, let him hear. ¹⁰ He who leads into captivity shall go into captivity; he who kills with the sword must be killed with the sword. Here is the patience and the faith of the saints.

(REVELATION 13:1–10)

What catches your attention from these verses? Why?

What are some key images in this passage? What do they communicate to you?

How does this passage contribute to your understanding of the Antichrist's nature? His goals?

What further connections do you see between these verses and Daniel's visions of the Antichrist that we explored in lesson 6?

The Antichrist will not operate alone. As we've already seen, he will be directly empowered by Satan as a twisted parallel to the Holy Spirit's empowering of Christ. Whatever the Antichrist speaks or achieves will be directly tied to his master, the Devil. As we continue exploring John's vision, we see another key player in the End Times drama—a second beast known as the False Prophet:

> [11] *Then I saw another beast coming up out of the earth, and he had two horns like a lamb and spoke like a dragon.* [12] *And he exercises all the authority of the first beast in his presence, and causes the earth and those who dwell in it to worship the first beast, whose deadly wound was healed.* [13] *He performs great signs, so that he even makes fire come down from heaven on the earth in the sight of men.* [14] *And he deceives those who dwell on the earth by those signs which he was granted to do in the sight of the beast, telling those who dwell on the earth to make an image to the beast who was wounded by the sword and lived.* [15] *He was granted power to give breath to the image of the beast, that the image of the beast should both speak and cause as many as would not worship the image of the beast to be killed.* [16] *He causes all, both small and great, rich and poor, free and slave, to receive a mark on their right hand or on their foreheads,* [17] *and that no one may buy or sell except one who has the mark or the name of the beast, or the number of his name.*
>
> [18] *Here is wisdom. Let him who has understanding calculate the number of the beast, for it is the number of a man: His number is 666.*
>
> (REVELATION 13:11–18)

How does John describe the appearance of this second beast?

What can we say for certain about the False Prophet based on these verses?

John describes the "mark of the beast" in verses 16–18. What are some possible ways this prophecy could play out in everyday life during the Tribulation?

How would you describe the interaction and relationships between the Dragon (Satan), the first beast (the Antichrist), and the second beast (the False Prophet)?

In lesson 6, we studied the opening of the first six seals of God's judgment as described in Revelation 6. The seventh seal is a transitional moment, initiating another wave of God's judgment that will be symbolized by seven trumpets. At the beginning of the Great Tribulation, the angels of heaven will blow the trumpets, sounding the alarm, for God is about to pour out the full fury of His wrath:

> 8:7 *The first angel sounded: And hail and fire followed, mingled with blood, and they were thrown to the earth. And a third of the trees were burned up, and all green grass was burned up.*
> 8 *Then the second angel sounded: And something like a great mountain burning with fire was thrown into the sea, and a third of the sea became blood. 9 And a third of the living creatures in the sea died, and a third of the ships were destroyed.*

[10] *Then the third angel sounded: And a great star fell from heaven, burning like a torch, and it fell on a third of the rivers and on the springs of water.* [11] *The name of the star is Wormwood. A third of the waters became wormwood, and many men died from the water, because it was made bitter.*

[12] *Then the fourth angel sounded: And a third of the sun was struck, a third of the moon, and a third of the stars, so that a third of them were darkened. A third of the day did not shine, and likewise the night.*

[13] *And I looked, and I heard an angel flying through the midst of heaven, saying with a loud voice, "Woe, woe, woe to the inhabitants of the earth, because of the remaining blasts of the trumpet of the three angels who are about to sound!"*

[9:1] *Then the fifth angel sounded: And I saw a star fallen from heaven to the earth. To him was given the key to the bottomless pit.* [2] *And he opened the bottomless pit, and smoke arose out of the pit like the smoke of a great furnace. So the sun and the air were darkened because of the smoke of the pit.* [3] *Then out of the smoke locusts came upon the earth. And to them was given power, as the scorpions of the earth have power.* [4] *They were commanded not to harm the grass of the earth, or any green thing, or any tree, but only those men who do not have the seal of God on their foreheads.* [5] *And they were not given authority to kill them, but to torment them for five months. Their torment was like the torment of a scorpion when it strikes a man.* [6] *In those days men will seek death and will not find it; they will desire to die, and death will flee from them.*

[7] *The shape of the locusts was like horses prepared for battle. On their heads were crowns of something like gold, and their faces were like the faces of men.* [8] *They had hair like women's hair, and their teeth were like lions' teeth.* [9] *And they had breastplates like breastplates of iron, and the sound of their wings was like the sound of chariots with many horses running into battle.* [10] *They had tails like scorpions, and there were stings in their tails. Their power was to hurt men five months.* [11] *And they had as king over them the angel of the bottomless pit, whose name in Hebrew is Abaddon, but in Greek he has the name Apollyon.*

[12] *One woe is past. Behold, still two more woes are coming after these things.*

[13] *Then the sixth angel sounded: And I heard a voice from the four horns of the golden altar which is before God,* [14] *saying to the sixth angel who had the trumpet, "Release the four angels who are bound at the great river Euphrates."* [15] *So the four angels, who had been prepared for the hour and day and month and year, were released to kill a third of mankind.* [16] *Now the number of the army of the horsemen*

was two hundred million; I heard the number of them. [17] *And thus I saw the horses in the vision: those who sat on them had breastplates of fiery red, hyacinth blue, and sulfur yellow; and the heads of the horses were like the heads of lions; and out of their mouths came fire, smoke, and brimstone.* [18] *By these three plagues a third of mankind was killed—by the fire and the smoke and the brimstone which came out of their mouths.* [19] *For their power is in their mouth and in their tails; for their tails are like serpents, having heads; and with them they do harm.*

[20] *But the rest of mankind, who were not killed by these plagues, did not repent of the works of their hands, that they should not worship demons, and idols of gold, silver, brass, stone, and wood, which can neither see nor hear nor walk.* [21] *And they did not repent of their murders or their sorceries or their sexual immorality or their thefts.*

(REVELATION 8:7–9:21)

What strikes you as especially noteworthy from these verses? Why?

How would you summarize the judgment initiated by the first six trumpet blasts? What will occur during each one?

- The first trumpet (Revelation 8:7):

- The second trumpet (Revelation 8:8–9):

- The third trumpet (Revelation 8:10–11):

- The fourth trumpet (Revelation 8:12–13):

- The fifth trumpet (Revelation 9:1–12):

- The sixth trumpet (Revelation 9:13–21):

Try to imagine what the world will be like in the midst of these calamities. How do you imagine the people in your community will respond?

Where do you see some of these calamities foreshadowed by recent headlines in the news? Explain.

Reflect on the Scripture

As a reminder, the Antichrist is a future world ruler who will govern ten nations, make and break a peace treaty with Israel, and later become dictator over the entire earth. Although the Antichrist will come to the forefront under a banner of peace and tolerance, he soon reveals his true colors. This Prince of Darkness will persecute those who do not accept his mark, cunningly created to allegedly solve the global economic problems.

The Antichrist will portray those who refuse to take his mark or swear allegiance to him as dangerous subversives. His campaign of terror against Jews and Christians (those who accept Christ as Lord after the Rapture) will escalate as he condemns Judeo Christian-based worship in all its forms. Satan's messiah will stop the daily sacrifices in the newly rebuilt holy temple in Jerusalem and will demand that he be worshiped as God as he establishes his New Age concept of a one-world religion.

The Antichrist will once again attack God's plan by making Jerusalem his seat of power. Why? Because Jerusalem is a living testimonial to Jews and Christians alike. We are sheltered in the arms of God just as His Holy City is cradled by the surrounding mountains and defended by God Himself. Knowing all this, the Antichrist will center his religious cult in Jerusalem, to include the very heart of the temple itself. He will know full well that his actions are an affront to Almighty God and His Chosen people, the Jews.

The Antichrist will not be alone in enacting his diabolical deeds. He will have an assistant who is as thoroughly committed to evil as he is. Remember this principle: Satan loves to mimic God's truth. He will continue doing so until the End of the Age and after. Thus, the Antichrist will be part of a perverted satanic trinity that will endeavor to function in much the same way as the Father, Son, and Holy Spirit. Satan, the first person of this evil triune, will supply power to the Antichrist, who will be aided by the deceitful False Prophet.

It is written in the Scriptures that the vast majority of people who are living during the Tribulation will submit to, and even worship, the Antichrist and his False Prophet. What evidence from history has displayed the same behavior?

The Word of God warns that any people who reject the Antichrist or his systems of governance will be cut off from society, imprisoned, and executed. Where do you see evidence from today's world that such things could take place?

Where do you see specific evidence of Satan's work in the world today?

The Antichrist will be in full control of the world as the Lord begins to pour out His wrath on the billions of people not taken up to heaven by the Rapture—specifically, those who rejected His free gift of salvation. As we've seen, the judgments initiated by the seven trumpets will be calamitous. Like nothing the world has ever seen.

Yet they will not be the end. The final set of judgments described in Revelation arrive with the Seven Vials (see Revelation 16:1–21). A vial is a bowl, and these Seven Bowls of fierce judgment will be poured out in rapid succession at the end of the Great Tribulation. As the Seventh Seal introduced the Seven Trumpet judgments, so the Seventh Trumpet judgment will introduce the Seven Bowl judgments.

The Seven Bowl judgments are similar to the trumpet judgments; however, whereas the trumpet judgments are partial in their effects, the bowl judgments will be complete and final. The seventh and final bowl judgment will signal the great battle of Armageddon and foretell the final ruin of the Antichrist. More than one-half of the world's population will die in the Tribulation, yet the remainder will persist in idolatry, immorality, and rebellion against God.

Read about the Seven Bowl judgments in Revelation 16:1–21. What will occur in each of those judgments?

- The first bowl (verse 2):

- The second bowl (verse 3):

- The third bowl (verses 4–7):

- The fourth bowl (verses 8–9):

- The fifth bowl (verses 10–11):

- The sixth bowl (verses 12–16):

- The seventh bowl (verses 17–21):

What emotions do you experience when you read those verses? Why?

Why is it necessary for God to pour out His wrath in this way? What is the purpose of these judgments?

What can we learn about God's character from these judgments?

Why is it significant that God has offered advanced warnings about these judgments and the things yet to come?

Act in Faith

The Tribulation will be a season of horror, but the good news is that those who have been redeemed by the Blood of the Lamb will not endure this tormenting time. We have been set free and whom the Son sets free is free indeed! Before Christ entered our lives, we were slaves to sin. But by God's grace, mercy and forgiveness we can now walk freely and speak boldly of the One who has given us the promise of eternal life with Him in heaven.

What are some words that characterize your life before you encountered Christ?

What are some words that characterize your life since encountering Christ?

Where have you felt the struggle against sin most keenly?

Where have you seen victory and transformation within that struggle?

Responsive Prayer: *Lord Jesus, I affirm the truth of Scripture that the wages of sin is death, but Your gift is eternal life. Thank You, my Savior, for that gift! Thank You, Lord Jesus, for Your sacrifice! Thank You for the transforming work You have accomplished and will continue to accomplish in my life. Amen.*

11:57 PM

Inching Toward Armageddon

And I saw the beast, the kings of the earth, and their armies, gathered together to make war against Him who sat on the horse and against His army. Then the beast was captured, and with him the false prophet who worked signs in his presence.

Revelation 19:19–20

Unlike Jesus Christ, whose throne will know no end, the Antichrist's days are numbered. While God readies the armies of heaven, the nations of earth will rise against the Antichrist.

From Chapter 8 of *The End of the Age*

The Battle of Gettysburg is widely considered the most consequential engagement of the United States Civil War— and with good reason. The battle, which stretched over three sweltering summer days on the plains of Pennsylvania, was filled with harrowing hesitancies, courageous charges, and strategic stands. Ultimately, those three days defined the future of a nation.

Robert E. Lee was at the head of the Confederate Army. Bolstered by a convincing victory over Union forces in Chancellorsville, Virginia, Lee decided to press his advantage and invade the northern states. He marched his troops into Pennsylvania until they met a Union army near Gettysburg on July 1, 1863.

The Union forces were led by General George G. Meade, whom Abraham Lincoln had appointed as Commander of the Army of the Potomac just *three days* before the battle took place. Meade immediately established strong defensive positions in the town of Gettysburg and the surrounding areas, including elevated areas such as Little Round Top.

On the third day of fighting, General Lee ordered what historians now refer to as Pickett's Charge. Nearly 15,000 Confederate troops marched three-quarters of a mile across open plains to attack Union positions that were secure behind stone walls. The charge failed. The battle was lost for Lee and the Confederate army, and the tide of the war was turned.

As we continue to count down the minutes on God's prophetic clock, we come to the most-talked-about battle that will ever be fought: Armageddon. Just as Gettysburg was a turning point in the Civil War, Armageddon will signal the beginning of the end for the prophetic period known as the Tribulation.

Explore the Scripture

Much like *Antichrist* and *Tribulation*, the word *Armageddon* is well known in our modern culture—yet not well understood. Most know that the term is connected to the end of the world. But it is often used to describe a cataclysmic event such as a nuclear war or a meteor strike.

In reality, Armageddon is a battle. In many ways, it will be *the* battle—the final struggle between good and evil before Christ establishes His Millennial Kingdom. Scripture contains several mentions of that future battle. In this lesson, we will piece together several of those different passages in order to paint a more complete picture of what will occur. For starters, let's explore what the prophet Zechariah wrote about that coming conflict:

> [2] *"Behold, I will make Jerusalem a cup of drunkenness to all the surrounding peoples, when they lay siege against Judah and Jerusalem.* [3] *And it shall happen in that day that I will make Jerusalem a very heavy stone for all peoples; all who would heave it away will surely be cut in pieces, though all nations of the earth are gathered against it.* [4] *In that day," says the LORD, "I will strike every horse with confusion, and its rider with madness; I will open My eyes on the house of Judah, and will strike every horse of the peoples with blindness.* [5] *And the governors of Judah shall say in their heart, 'The inhabitants of Jerusalem are my strength in the LORD of hosts, their God.'* [6] *In that day I will make the governors of Judah like a firepan in the woodpile, and like a fiery torch in the sheaves; they shall devour all the surrounding peoples on the right hand and on the left, but Jerusalem shall be inhabited again in her own place—Jerusalem.*
>
> [7] *"The LORD will save the tents of Judah first, so that the glory of the house of David and the glory of the inhabitants of Jerusalem shall not become greater than that of Judah.* [8] *In that day the LORD will defend the inhabitants of Jerusalem; the one who is feeble among them in that day shall be like David, and the house of David shall be like God, like the Angel of the LORD before them.* [9] *It shall be in that day that I will seek to destroy all the nations that come against Jerusalem.*
>
> [10] *"And I will pour on the house of David and on the inhabitants of Jerusalem the Spirit of grace and supplication; then they will look on Me whom they pierced. Yes, they will mourn for Him as one mourns for his only son, and grieve for Him as one grieves for a firstborn.* [11] *In that day there shall be a great mourning in Jerusalem, like the mourning at Hadad Rimmon in the plain of Megiddo.* [12] *And the land shall mourn, every family by itself: the family of the house of David by itself, and their wives by themselves; the family of the house of Nathan by itself, and their wives by themselves;* [13] *the family of the house of Levi by itself, and their wives by themselves; the family of Shimei by itself, and their wives by themselves;* [14] *all the families that remain, every family by itself, and their wives by themselves.*

(ZECHARIAH 12:2–14)

How would you describe the overall tone or tenor of these verses?

What are some key images contained in this passage? What do they communicate to you?

What are some specific consequences that will come about after the battle of Armageddon?

- Consequences for Jerusalem:

- Consequences for the nations of the world:

- Consequences for the Jewish people:

How would you describe God's role before, during, and after this battle?

The book of Revelation also contains prophecies connected to this important battle. Most critically, John's vision reveals the role Christ will play in securing the ultimate victory against Satan, the Antichrist, and the False Prophet:

[11] *Now I saw heaven opened, and behold, a white horse. And He who sat on him was called Faithful and True, and in righteousness He judges and makes war.* [12] *His eyes were like a flame of fire, and on His head were many crowns. He had*

*a name written that no one knew except Himself. *[13]* He was clothed with a robe dipped in blood, and His name is called The Word of God. *[14]* And the armies in heaven, clothed in fine linen, white and clean, followed Him on white horses. *[15]* Now out of His mouth goes a sharp sword, that with it He should strike the nations. And He Himself will rule them with a rod of iron. He Himself treads the winepress of the fierceness and wrath of Almighty God. *[16]* And He has on His robe and on His thigh a name written:*

KING OF KINGS AND
LORD OF LORDS.

[17] Then I saw an angel standing in the sun; and he cried with a loud voice, saying to all the birds that fly in the midst of heaven, "Come and gather together for the supper of the great God, *[18]* that you may eat the flesh of kings, the flesh of captains, the flesh of mighty men, the flesh of horses and of those who sit on them, and the flesh of all people, free and slave, both small and great."*
[19] And I saw the beast, the kings of the earth, and their armies, gathered together to make war against Him who sat on the horse and against His army. *[20]* Then the beast was captured, and with him the false prophet who worked signs in his presence, by which he deceived those who received the mark of the beast and those who worshiped his image. These two were cast alive into the lake of fire burning with brimstone. *[21]* And the rest were killed with the sword which proceeded from the mouth of Him who sat on the horse. And all the birds were filled with their flesh.*

(REVELATION 19:11–21)

What do you like best about these verses? Why?

What are some of the key images contained in these verses?

How does this vision add to your understanding of Armageddon? What can you say for certain about it based on this passage?

What do these verses reveal about Jesus' nature? His character?

Reflect on the Scripture

Based on the total scope of biblical prophecy, there is strong reason to believe the battle of Armageddon will proceed in four distinct steps.

First, a coalition of nations will rebel against the Antichrist. Even though the Antichrist will establish a one-world system of government, his rule will only endure for a matter of years. In addition, many nations and leaders who are forced to bow their knee, will do so grudgingly. In the chaos of the Tribulation, at least one army will form with the intent to overthrow Satan's hand-chosen ruler.

The book of Daniel offers a prophetic look at this confrontation:

40 At the time of the end the king of the South shall attack him; and the king of the North shall come against him like a whirlwind, with chariots, horsemen, and with many ships; and he shall enter the countries, overwhelm them, and pass through. 41 He shall also enter the Glorious Land, and many countries shall be overthrown; but these shall escape from his hand: Edom, Moab, and the prominent people of Ammon. 42 He shall stretch out his hand against the countries, and the land of Egypt shall not escape. 43 He shall have power over the treasures of gold and silver, and over all the precious things of Egypt; also the Libyans and Ethiopians shall follow at his heels.

(REVELATION 11:40–43)

The second step will occur as the Antichrist publicly and continually speaks blasphemies against God. In Revelation 13:6, John writes that the Antichrist will open "his mouth in blasphemy against God, to blaspheme His name, His tabernacle, and those who dwell in heaven."

Part of this blasphemy will include another attempt to exterminate the Jewish people. Why? Because they are beloved of God, and because Satan has always sought their destruction. Having gained control of Jerusalem, the Antichrist will be in an ideal position to strike the apple of God's eye.

Yet his blow will have to wait. The third step leading up to the battle of Armageddon will involve God drawing the armies of the world near Jerusalem to the plains of Megiddo. In Joel 3:2, God said, "I will also gather all nations, and bring them down to the Valley of Jehoshaphat." As we saw earlier from Zechariah, God said, "Behold, I will make Jerusalem a cup of drunkenness to all the surrounding peoples, when they lay siege against Judah and Jerusalem. . . . I will gather all the nations to battle" (Zechariah 12:2; 14:2).

The battle of Armageddon will begin on the plains of Megiddo to the north, continue down through the Valley of Jehoshaphat on the east, cover the land of Edom to the south and east, and revolve around Jerusalem. Fighting will begin almost immediately. The Antichrist's enemies will lay siege to Jerusalem, then overrun her city defenses and wreak the havoc as Zechariah so vividly described. They will take captives, murder, rape, and pillage until the streets run red with blood.

Already engaged in battle, the Antichrist will be confronted with a new threat: China. As we read, "But news from the east and the north shall trouble him; therefore he shall go out with great fury to destroy and annihilate many. And he shall plant the tents of his palace between the seas and the glorious holy mountain; yet he shall come to his end, and no one will help him" (Revelation 11:44–45). An army of 200 million soldiers will advance from China and attempt to seize the Persian Gulf. As a result, the Antichrist will advance from the territory of the defeated king of the South to Armageddon, a natural battlefield, to face the armies of the North and East.

The fourth and final step of Armageddon will be unveiled with a final wave of attack—not from any earthly army, but from the forces of heaven. This is the invasion described in Revelation 19, which will be led by Christ riding His white horse. The King of kings will descend onto the battlefield. As He comes, His eyes will be like blazing fire, and the armies of heaven will follow Him. Out of the Messiah's mouth will come a sharp, two-edged sword—the Word of God with which He created the world, raised Lazarus from the dead, and rebuked the unruly wind and waves on the Sea of Galilee. This very same spoken Word will crush Israel's enemies at Armageddon—and of His Kingdom there shall be no end!

What advantage do Christians gain by becoming aware of these events ahead of time?

How would you define "blasphemy" in today's language? What is it and why is it so destructive?

Satan and the Antichrist will both attempt to exterminate God's chosen people, the Jews. How should Christians view the Jewish people? The Jewish nation?

What are specific ways that Christians have benefitted from the history and culture of the Jewish people?

Read Judges 7:1–25 to explore another battle that occurred on or around the plains of Megiddo thousands of years ago. What are the similarities and differences between Gideon's defeat of the Midianites and Christ's victory at Armageddon?

Act in Faith

As we have seen through the vivid description of God's Word, the Tribulation will be a season of terror for mankind. The Antichrist will be more dangerous, more calculating, and more powerful than any other leader who has ever ascended to any throne. In the coming conflict, the threats against God's people—both those on earth and those in heaven—will be dreadful to behold.

And yet, we need not fear. We need not even blink an eye or hold our breath in worry. Why? Because Christ is victorious. The Savior of the world has already won the day, and our enemies are already defeated. That is the overwhelming message of Scripture. That is the never-ending promise of God's Word. You and I are on the winning team. Evil has been defeated, which means we can live and love and serve with confidence.

Read aloud 1 Corinthians 15:50–56 to conclude this lesson:

[50] *Now this I say, brethren, that flesh and blood cannot inherit the kingdom of God; nor does corruption inherit incorruption.* [51] *Behold, I tell you a mystery: We shall not all sleep, but we shall all be changed—* [52] *in a moment, in the twinkling of an eye, at the last trumpet. For the trumpet will sound, and the dead will be raised incorruptible, and we shall be changed.* [53] *For this corruptible must put on incorruption, and this mortal must put on immortality.* [54] *So when this corruptible has put on incorruption, and this mortal has put on immortality, then shall be brought to pass the saying that is written: "Death is swallowed up in victory."*

[55] *"O Death, where is your sting?*
O Hades, where is your victory?"

[56] *The sting of death is sin, and the strength of sin is the law.* [57] *But thanks be to God, who gives us the victory through our Lord Jesus Christ.*

How have you participated in Christ's victory over death?

Where do you see the fruits of Jesus' victory over sin in your life specifically? In the world at large?

What steps can you take this week to continually remind yourself of Christ's present and future victory?

Responsive Prayer: *Lord Jesus Christ, I affirm the truth of Your Word that death is swallowed up in victory! You have conquered sin. You have conquered the grave. And You have already conquered Satan and all his forces. Because of what You have done, Lord Jesus, I reject the sting of death. I reject the fear of death. I choose to live in the reality of Your victory, both now and for all eternity. Amen.*

11:58 PM

The Millennium Dawns

Then I saw an angel coming down from heaven, having the key to the bottomless pit and a great chain in his hand. He laid hold of the dragon, that serpent of old, who is the Devil and Satan, and bound him for a thousand years; and he cast him into the bottomless pit, and shut him up, and set a seal on him, so that he should deceive the nations no more till the thousand years were finished.

Revelation 20:1–3

Imagine if you will, a thousand years of Sabbath-like rest, genuine peace, perfect health and absolute worship. A place of true harmony where, "The wolf also shall dwell with the lamb, the leopard shall lie down with the young goat, the calf and the young lion and the fatling together; and a little child shall lead them" (Isaiah 11:6). These elements will all define the Millennial Reign.

From Chapter 9 of *The End of the Age*

95

Throughout history, mankind has been searching for utopia.
Utopia represents a perfect society—a place where everyone finds prosperity,
behaves appropriately, and achieves their version of happiness. Some chose to
explore the world in search of such a place . . . and never found what they were
seeking. Others attempted to build a utopian society, either by adapting and
enforcing laws in their current communities or by launching new settlements in
new places. All of those efforts failed.

The term *utopia* comes from the title of a book written by Thomas More in
the sixteenth century. The story unfolds as a series of letters about a small island
nation in South America called Utopia that exists as a perfect society. People are
grouped in regular cohorts rather than nuclear families. There are no personal
possessions or wealth. (Gold is used to make toilets so that people will not covet
it.) People change houses every ten years just to keep things fair. Every citizen
contributes to agriculture and at least one other trade.

If that sounds appealing, you should know that More's "perfect" society included several major flaws. Slavery was permitted with every family having two
slaves—foreigners captured from other countries or prisoners who committed
crimes. Premarital sex was punished by a lifetime of forced celibacy. Euthanasia
was common, and women were required to confess their sins to their husbands
every month.

Importantly, Thomas More—who was a devoted Catholic—was not attempting to create a perfect human society. Instead, he was highlighting the fact that
no perfect society has existed or ever will exist. Indeed, More created the word
utopia to reveal that truth. It is a combination of the Greek word *ou* ("not") with
topos ("place"). In other words, utopia is literally translated as "nowhere." More
understood the reality of human nature and the futility of seeking perfection
within a corrupted culture.

There will never be a perfect society in a world still infected by sin. Yet we will
witness something close to perfection during the Millennium—the thousand-year
reign of Christ on earth after the final events of the Tribulation.

Explore the Scripture

What is the Millennial Kingdom of Christ? The Millennium is the reign of Christ
for one thousand years on the earth following His second coming. Although it is

not often preached from Sunday pulpits, the Millennium is mentioned frequently in the Bible. It is known in Scripture as "the world to come" (Hebrews 2:5), "the kingdom of heaven" (Matthew 5:10), "the kingdom of God" (Mark 1:14), "the last day" (John 6:40), and "the regeneration" (Matthew 19:28). Jesus told His disciples, "Assuredly I say to you, that in the regeneration, when the Son of Man sits on the throne of His glory, you who have followed Me will also sit on twelve thrones, judging the twelve tribes of Israel" (Matthew 19:28).

The Millennium was foreshadowed in the Old Testament by the Sabbath, a biblical time of rest. The Sabbath was observed after six workdays, six work weeks, six work months, and six work years. In God's eternal plan, the earth will rest after six thousand years as well, from the time of Creation until the End of the Age, as He ushers in the Millennial Kingdom of the Messiah.

The Millennium will also be a time of rest for the people of God. As we read in Hebrews 4:8–10, "For if Joshua had given them rest, then He would not afterward have spoken of another day. There remains therefore a rest for the people of God. For he who has entered His rest has himself also ceased from his works as God did from His." A rest of grace, comfort, and holiness will be available through the eternal Sabbath of heaven, where believers will enjoy the object of all their desires. We will enter into this rest just like God the Father and Christ, our Redeemer, entered their glorious rest.

John's vision in the book of Revelation also includes a vivid picture of Christ's Millennial Kingdom:

> [1] *Then I saw an angel coming down from heaven, having the key to the bottomless pit and a great chain in his hand.* [2] *He laid hold of the dragon, that serpent of old, who is the Devil and Satan, and bound him for a thousand years;* [3] *and he cast him into the bottomless pit, and shut him up, and set a seal on him, so that he should deceive the nations no more till the thousand years were finished. But after these things he must be released for a little while.*
>
> [4] *And I saw thrones, and they sat on them, and judgment was committed to them. Then I saw the souls of those who had been beheaded for their witness to Jesus and for the word of God, who had not worshiped the beast or his image, and had not received his mark on their foreheads or on their hands. And they lived and reigned with Christ for a thousand years.* [5] *But the rest of the dead did not live again until the thousand years were finished. This is the first resurrection.* [6] *Blessed and*

holy is he who has part in the first resurrection. Over such the second death has no power, but they shall be priests of God and of Christ, and shall reign with Him a thousand years.

(REVELATION 20:1–6)

What elements of this passage feel especially hopeful to you? Why?

Satan and his forces will be chained away during the Millennial Kingdom. How does Satan influence and interact with our world today?

What are some ways the world will be different without Satan's influence or corruption?

What are some ways it will be similar to today?

How should we understand the word *reign* in verse 6?

During the Millennium, the geography of Israel will be dramatically changed. Israel will be greatly enlarged, and for the first time, Israel will possess all the land promised to Abraham in Genesis 15:18–21, which includes all of present-day Israel, all of Lebanon, half of Syria, two-thirds of Jordan, all of Iraq, and the northern portion of Saudi Arabia. Moreover, the desert will become a fertile plain, and a miraculous river will flow east to west from the Mount of Olives into both the Mediterranean and the Dead Sea—but this salted sea will be dead no longer!

Jerusalem, the city of God, will be the center of this Millennial Kingdom. Christ will establish His seat and reign from God's Holy City. Look at how the prophet Micah describes the glory of Jerusalem during the Millennium:

> [1] *Now it shall come to pass in the latter days*
> *That the mountain of the Lord's house*
> *Shall be established on the top of the mountains,*
> *And shall be exalted above the hills;*
> *And peoples shall flow to it.*
> [2] *Many nations shall come and say,*
> *"Come, and let us go up to the mountain of the Lord,*
> *To the house of the God of Jacob;*
> *He will teach us His ways,*
> *And we shall walk in His paths."*
> *For out of Zion the law shall go forth,*
> *And the word of the Lord from Jerusalem.*
> [3] *He shall judge between many peoples,*
> *And rebuke strong nations afar off;*
> *They shall beat their swords into plowshares,*
> *And their spears into pruning hooks;*
> *Nation shall not lift up sword against nation,*
> *Neither shall they learn war anymore.*

⁴ But everyone shall sit under his vine and under his fig tree,
And no one shall make them afraid;
For the mouth of the LORD of hosts has spoken.
⁵ For all people walk each in the name of his god,
But we will walk in the name of the LORD our God
Forever and ever.

(MICAH 4:1–5)

What strikes you as most interesting or noteworthy from these verses? Why?

Based on these verses, what can you say for certain about the Millennial Kingdom?

How do these verses paint a different picture than the Antichrist's reign, which we explored in the previous two lessons?

How do these verses paint a different picture than what you have experienced throughout your lifetime?

Reflect on the Scripture

We have not yet fully addressed the most important factor in Christ's Millennial Kingdom—Christ Himself! This period of a thousand years will be glorious, restful and filled with joy. But those things will only be true because *Jesus* will be at the center of it all. Indeed, Jesus will officially take His rightful place as the center of everything. Remember, Scripture emphasizes again and again that Jesus is the rightful King not only of heaven or some vague "spiritual realm" but also over all of creation. He is Lord of all!

For instance, in Genesis 49 we read that Jacob the patriarch called his twelve sons around his deathbed to give them a final blessing and to speak a prophetic word over each of them. His word over Judah was especially insightful: "Judah, you are he whom your brothers shall praise; your hand shall be on the neck of your enemies; your father's children shall bow down before you. . . . The scepter shall not depart from Judah, nor a lawgiver from between his feet, until Shiloh comes" (verses 8, 10). The word *Shiloh* may be translated as "He whose right it is to rule." Jacob thus prophesied that a man who had the right to be king would come from Judah's lineage—which is true of Jesus!

Perhaps the most famous prophesy about Jesus' kingship can be found in 2 Samuel 7, when God spoke these words through the prophet Nathan:

> [12] *"When your days are fulfilled and you rest with your fathers, I will set up your seed after you, who will come from your body, and I will establish his kingdom.* [13] *He shall build a house for My name, and I will establish the throne of his kingdom forever.* [14] *I will be his Father, and he shall be My son. If he commits iniquity, I will chasten him with the rod of men and with the blows of the sons of men.* [15] *But My mercy shall not depart from him, as I took it from Saul, whom I removed from before you.* [16] *And your house and your kingdom shall be established forever before you. Your throne shall be established forever."*

(2 SAMUEL 7:12–16)

Of course, the angel Gabriel spoke this prophecy to Mary when he announced that she would become pregnant with the Messiah:

> *"Do not be afraid, Mary, for you have found favor with God. And behold, you will conceive in your womb and bring forth a Son, and shall call His name Jesus. He*

will be great, and will be called the Son of the Highest; and the Lord God will give Him the throne of His father David. And He will reign over the house of Jacob forever, and of His kingdom there will be no end."

(LUKE 1:30–33)

What does it mean to recognize Jesus as "king" in today's world?

How will that recognition change during the Millennial Kingdom? What will be different?

What does it look like for you personally to acknowledge Christ as your king? How does His kingship impact:

- Your spiritual life?

- Your work and career?

- Your finances?

- Your family?

Read Jesus' Parable of the Talents in Matthew 25:14–30. What can you learn from this parable about your role in the coming Millennial Kingdom?

Another topic that we have not yet addressed is the question of *why*. What is the purpose of the Millennium in terms of God's plan for history? God has several reasons for instituting an earthly kingdom over which His Son will reign.

First, He has promised to reward His children. As we just read in the Parable of the Talents, "Then the King will say to those on His right hand, 'Come, you blessed of My Father, inherit the kingdom prepared for you from the foundation of the world' " (Matthew 25:34).

Second, God promised Abraham that Israel would become a mighty nation, which has already come to pass, and that his seed would someday own the Promised Land forever (see Genesis 12:7; 13:14–17). This is not the somewhat isolated plot of land we currently recognize as the nation of Israel, but the entirety of God's "promised land." During the Millennial reign of Christ, Israel will be expanded to fulfill the full measure of God's covenant promise to Abraham and Moses.

Third, God will establish the Millennial Kingdom to fulfill the prayers of His children. When Jesus taught His disciples the model prayer, or the Lord's Prayer, He told them to pray, "Your kingdom come" (Luke 11:1–4). The phrase "Your kingdom come" isn't just a little ditty meant to rhyme with "Your will be done"; it is a plea that God would soon establish His earthly and eternal Kingdom!

Finally, God will establish His Millennial Kingdom to prove a point. In the Millennium, God will redeem creation, resulting in the existence of docile wild animals, plentiful crops, and the purest of water. The world will know one thousand years of peace, joy, holiness, glory, comfort, justice, health, protection, freedom, and prosperity. Satan will be bound and not able to wreak havoc on earth. King Jesus Himself will rule from Jerusalem, and immortal believers with godly wisdom will rule other cities.

But despite this near utopia, man's fallen nature will still pull him into sin and disobedience. The Millennium will be a one-thousand-year lesson of man's ultimate moral corruption. The secular humanistic idea that man can improve himself to the point of perfection will be proven false once and for all; the concept of pseudo-paradise will vanish like the morning mist.

How will the Millennial Kingdom serve as a reward for those who follow Christ? What will we receive?

What are you most looking forward to about this thousand-year period? Why?

How does our culture view the inherent "goodness" or "wickedness" of human beings?

Where do you see evidence for those traits?

- Goodness:

- Wickedness:

Act in Faith

Let's return to an important truth about our role as followers of Jesus during the Millennial Kingdom. Namely, we will participate in Christ's kingship. The apostle Paul said it this way:

This is a faithful saying: For if we died with Him, we shall also live with Him. If we endure, we shall also reign with Him.

(2 TIMOTHY 2:11–12).

Don't lose sight of that amazing truth! You and I will have the opportunity to reign with Jesus during the Millennium. We will have responsibility, authority, and purpose. We will exercise a role in the governmental operation of God's Kingdom for a thousand years.

Do you feel prepared for such a role? If not, remember it is your birthright. It is what you were created for, just as Adam was handcrafted to be a faithful steward of the Garden he inherited: "Then God said, 'Let Us make man in Our image, according to Our likeness; let them have dominion over the fish of the sea, over the birds of the air, and over the cattle, over all the earth and over every creeping thing that creeps on the earth'" (Genesis 1:26).

Read again these words from the Parable of the Talents:

²⁰ *"So he who had received five talents came and brought five other talents, saying, 'Lord, you delivered to me five talents; look, I have gained five more talents besides them.' ²¹ His lord said to him, 'Well done, good and faithful servant; you were faithful over a few things, I will make you ruler over many things. Enter*

into the joy of your lord.' [22] He also who had received two talents came and said, 'Lord, you delivered to me two talents; look, I have gained two more talents besides them.' [23] His lord said to him, 'Well done, good and faithful servant; you have been faithful over a few things, I will make you ruler over many things. Enter into the joy of your lord.'"

(MATTHEW 25:20–23)

What are some of the primary resources (talents) that you have been given during your time on earth?

In what ways have you been a faithful steward of those resources?

Where would you like to improve in your stewardship of what you've been given?

What specific steps can you take over the next year to better prepare yourself as a future steward of Christ's Millennial Kingdom?

Responsive Prayer: *Lord Jesus, I desire to hear You say, "Well done, good and faithful servant." I deeply long to share in the joy of my Lord. I understand that being labeled a faithful servant in the future means living as a faithful servant in the present, and I commit to that life. The resources You have given me are Yours, and I will use them in Your kingdom for Your glory. Amen.*

11:59 PM

The Earth's Final Conflict

Now when the thousand years have expired, Satan will be released from his prison and will go out to deceive the nations which are in the four corners of the earth, Gog and Magog, to gather them together to battle, whose number is as the sand of the sea.

Revelation 20:7–8

At the end of the Millennium, Satan will be loosed from his prison, and thousands of people from all the nations of the earth will believe his lies and follow him once again. They will gather around Jerusalem, Christ's capital city, and wage a great war. . . . where Jesus rules and reigns.

From Chapter 10 of *The End of the Age*

March 20, 1815, was a day of triumph for Napoleon Bonaparte. A return to glory. Just three weeks before, the famous French general had escaped from his exiled confinement on the island of Elba. After landing at the coastal city of Cannes, he rallied a number of peasants in the countryside to his cause. Then, when a regiment of soldiers was sent to arrest him, he won their hearts as well. They became part of his growing army.

It was on March 20 that Napoleon returned to Paris. He entered the city with great pomp and circumstance, once again declaring himself emperor of France. By that time, the recently re-instated King Louis XVIII had fled the city and was in hiding, terrified that the old conqueror would find him and destroy him.

The emperor's glorious return was remarkable for several reasons. For one thing, Napoleon had suffered a devastating defeat just three years earlier when he attempted to invade Russia. He led an army of 600,000 men across the frozen plains toward Moscow. The majority of those forces did not return. Humbled, Napoleon spent the next year reasserting control over his empire in Europe, but he had been diminished. Fighting wars on multiple fronts, he abdicated his throne in April 1814 and accepted exile to Elba, arriving at that island on May 4.

But that was in the past! Now, less than a year later, Napoleon was once again in Paris and once again determined to bend all of Europe to his will. Fortunately for history, the rest of Europe was not as accommodating as the French capital. When Britain and other allies raised up an army to confront him, Napoleon marched into Belgium to press the attack. He was ready to redeem his disastrous campaign in Russia. He believed this moment would be different. This time the outcome would bring unquestioned glory.

He was wrong. Napoleon was defeated soundly on June 18, 1815, at the Battle of Waterloo. He fled to Paris, where he was once again forced to abdicate his throne. A month later, he boarded the British vessel Bellerophon and was exiled to a second island—this one called St. Helena in the South Atlantic. There were no more escapes. No more glorious campaigns. Napoleon's brief return to splendor lasted a mere 100 days. He died quietly years later at the age of 51.[1]

Like Napoleon, Satan will endure a humiliating defeat at the end of the Tribulation. He will be struck down and captured by Jesus the King, the Rider on the white horse. He will be bound and thrown into prison for a thousand years. But, Satan's story will not end there.

Explore the Scripture

John's vision in the book of Revelation describes a final battle between good and evil at the end of history. This battle will occur after Satan is released from his millennium-long imprisonment, and it will result in total judgment against and eradication of sin. *But wait!* you might think. *How can Satan flourish after the Tribulation? How can he gather forces after Christ has reigned for a thousand years? Who will be left to follow the Devil?*

The answer is that millions of babies will be born during this thousand-year period. They will be babies just like you and I once were—prone to sin and bent toward trouble. Although the Christian parents who enter the Millennium will teach their children right from wrong, some of these children will exercise their free will and choose to do wrong. Some of them, as Zechariah tells us, will "not come up to Jerusalem to worship the King, the Lord of hosts," so on them "there will be no rain" (Zechariah 14:17).

The key to remember is that Christ's Millennial Kingdom will not be *heaven*. It will not be a perfect kingdom in the heavenly realm where sin and pain and death do not exist—that comes later. Instead, the Millennial Kingdom will be similar to what Adam and Eve experienced in the Garden of Eden. People will have the chance to walk and talk with Jesus, the King. He will be present among them on the earth. Yet people will still possess the ability to sin by rebelling against His rule, just as Adam and Eve possessed the ability to reject God's commands even though they were as yet untainted by sin.

One of the main differences between the Garden of Eden and the Millennial Kingdom is that Satan will be *chained*. He will not be allowed to spread deception in and through the people of the world. But that will change when the thousand years comes to an end. Here is what Scripture says about that time:

> [7] *Now when the thousand years have expired, Satan will be released from his prison* [8] *and will go out to deceive the nations which are in the four corners of the earth, Gog and Magog, to gather them together to battle, whose number is as the sand of the sea.* [9] *They went up on the breadth of the earth and surrounded the camp of the saints and the beloved city. And fire came down from God out of heaven and devoured them.* [10] *The devil, who deceived them, was cast into the lake of fire and brimstone where the beast and the false prophet are. And they will be tormented day and night forever and ever.*

(REVELATION 20:7–10)

What questions come to mind as you read these verses?

What are some possible reasons for Satan's eventual release?

"The devil, who deceived them, was cast into the lake of fire and brimstone" (verse 10). What emotions do you feel when you contemplate that lake?

To better understand God's victory at the end of history, we need to seek a better understanding of our enemy, Satan. The following passages of Scripture offer specific insights into who Satan is and how he operates in our world. As you read each one, write down how that passage adds to your understanding of the Devil.

> [1] *Now the serpent was more cunning than any beast of the field which the LORD God had made. And he said to the woman, "Has God indeed said, 'You shall not eat of every tree of the garden'?"*
>
> [2] *And the woman said to the serpent, "We may eat the fruit of the trees of the garden;* [3] *but of the fruit of the tree which is in the midst of the garden, God has said, 'You shall not eat it, nor shall you touch it, lest you die.'"*

⁴ Then the serpent said to the woman, "You will not surely die. ⁵ For God knows that in the day you eat of it your eyes will be opened, and you will be like God, knowing good and evil."

⁶ So when the woman saw that the tree was good for food, that it was pleasant to the eyes, and a tree desirable to make one wise, she took of its fruit and ate. She also gave to her husband with her, and he ate. ⁷ Then the eyes of both of them were opened, and they knew that they were naked; and they sewed fig leaves together and made themselves coverings.

(GENESIS 3:1–7)

What can we learn about Satan from his temptation of Adam and Eve?

How have you experienced similar temptation in your life?

⁴² Jesus said to them, "If God were your Father, you would love Me, for I proceeded forth and came from God; nor have I come of Myself, but He sent Me. ⁴³ Why do you not understand My speech? Because you are not able to listen to My word. ⁴⁴ You are of your father the devil, and the desires of your father you want to do. He was a murderer from the beginning, and does not stand in the truth, because there is no truth in him. When he speaks a lie, he speaks from his own resources, for he is a liar and the father of it. ⁴⁵ But because I tell the truth, you do not believe Me.

(JOHN 8:42–45)

How do these verses add to your understanding of Satan's nature? His schemes?

What are some lies that have been roadblocks in your spiritual life?

[12] But what I do, I will also continue to do, that I may cut off the opportunity from those who desire an opportunity to be regarded just as we are in the things of which they boast. [13] For such are false apostles, deceitful workers, transforming themselves into apostles of Christ. [14] And no wonder! For Satan himself transforms himself into an angel of light. [15] Therefore it is no great thing if his ministers also transform themselves into ministers of righteousness, whose end will be according to their works.

(2 CORINTHIANS 11:12–15)

What do you remember about Satan's history as an "angel of light"?

On a practical level, what does it look like for Satan and his minions to "transform themselves into apostles of Christ"? How can you recognize false teachers?

Reflect on the Scripture

Although we don't fully understand why, the witness of Scripture makes it clear that our enemy, the Devil, will be released from his prison after a thousand years. This release will mark the beginning of the end for the Millennium—and, in many ways, the beginning of eternity.

In the same way that Napoleon gathered followers after escaping Elba and arriving on the shores of France, so Satan will attract thousands of people from all the nations of the earth. These people will believe his lies and willingly choose to align themselves as enemies of Christ. They will gather around Jerusalem, Christ's capital city, and wage a great war.

What will induce these people to follow Satan? As the prophet Jeremiah wrote, "The heart is deceitful above all things, and desperately wicked; who can know it?" (Jeremiah 17:9). Who can understand what drives us to sin? For those who are living in earthly bodies, even as we are now, the law of sin is like the law of gravity. No matter how much we want to rise above it, it draws us down. It is only through the power of Christ that we can rise above sin at all.

Whatever the cause, the sad reality is that under ideal circumstances—an abundant earth, no sickness, no war—the human heart will prove that it remains unchanged unless regenerated by the power of Christ. When Satan is loosed on the earth, many will turn their backs on God, who has sustained them in a perfect world. Against all reason, they will follow the evil one.

As an army, the followers of Satan will advance against Jerusalem. This will not be a "mass protest." This will not be an attempt to take hold of a city or forcefully eject the ruling class. Rather, this will be an attack against Christ Himself. This will be Satan's final move in his millennia-long war against God—an attempt to destroy God by any means necessary.

Obviously, the attempt will fail. As John wrote, "They went up on the breadth of the earth and surrounded the camp of the saints and the beloved city. And fire came down from God out of heaven and devoured them. The devil, who deceived them, was cast into the lake of fire and brimstone where the beast and the false prophet *are*. And they will be tormented day and night forever and ever" (Revelation 20:9–10). This will be God's physical judgment against sin. Everything touched by sin will be destroyed, including the earth itself.

The apostle Peter revealed this moment with striking imagery:

> ¹⁰ *But the day of the Lord will come as a thief in the night, in which the heavens will pass away with a great noise, and the elements will melt with fervent heat; both the earth and the works that are in it will be burned up.* ¹¹ *Therefore, since all these things will be dissolved, what manner of persons ought you to be in holy conduct and godliness,* ¹² *looking for and hastening the coming of the day of God, because of which the heavens will be dissolved, being on fire, and the elements will melt with fervent heat?* ¹³ *Nevertheless we, according to His promise, look for new heavens and a new earth in which righteousness dwells.*

(2 PETER 3:10–11)

How do Peter's words add to your understanding of the beginning of eternity?

How would you answer Peter's question in verse 11: "Since all these things will be dissolved, what manner of persons ought you to be in holy conduct and godliness?"

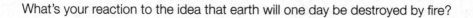

What's your reaction to the idea that earth will one day be destroyed by fire?

How does understanding the End of the Age help you to navigate your everyday life in the present?

What helps you find comfort in the future—both the future of the world, generally, and your future specifically?

Act in Faith

As we've seen in this lesson, understanding who Satan is and anticipating how he operates is important for resisting his efforts to cause harm. The Devil is a liar through and through, yet most of his deceptions are not violent or caustic. Instead, he deceptively presents himself as an angel of light—as someone trying to help us find freedom or gain something worthwhile.

How do we recognize and reject Satan's schemes? By keeping our eyes focused on Christ. The more we are connected to God through His Spirit, the more we will spot Satan's schemes—and the less appealing they will seem.

Still, it's important to remember that Satan does not work alone. For one thing, our enemy leads an army of spiritual beings who have eons of practice at tempting and attacking humanity. As Paul wrote, "For we do not wrestle against flesh and blood, but against principalities, against powers, against the rulers of the darkness of this age, against spiritual hosts of wickedness in the heavenly places. Therefore take up the whole armor of God, that you may be able to withstand in the evil day, and having done all, to stand" (Ephesians 6:12–13).

Beyond demons, however, Satan also works through *people*—through false teachers. Jesus spoke specifically about the role these corrupted humans will play during the events of the End of the Age:

> [4] *Take heed that no one deceives you.* [5] *For many will come in My name, saying, 'I am the Christ,' and will deceive many.* [6] *And you will hear of wars and rumors of wars. See that you are not troubled; for all these things must come to pass, but the end is not yet.* [7] *For nation will rise against nation, and kingdom against kingdom. And there will be famines, pestilences, and earthquakes in various places.* [8] *All these are the beginning of sorrows.*
>
> [9] *"Then they will deliver you up to tribulation and kill you, and you will be hated by all nations for My name's sake.* [10] *And then many will be offended, will betray one another, and will hate one another.* [11] *Then many false prophets will rise up and deceive many.* [12] *And because lawlessness will abound, the love of many will grow cold.* [13] *But he who endures to the end shall be saved.* [14] *And this gospel of the kingdom will be preached in all the world as a witness to all the nations, and then the end will come.*
>
> (MATTHEW 24:4–13)

All followers of Jesus have a responsibility to reject and counter the work of these false teachers. The first step in this fight is to avoid allowing ourselves to participate in false teaching. With this in mind, how confident do you feel in your understanding of the following critical doctrines?

- The message of the gospel—how to be saved:

1	2	3	4	5	6	7	8	9	10

(Not confident)   (Very confident)

- The doctrine of the Trinity—God as Father, Son, and Holy Spirit:

1	2	3	4	5	6	7	8	9	10

(Not confident)   (Very confident)

- The inspiration and inerrancy of God's Word:

1	2	3	4	5	6	7	8	9	10

(Not confident)   (Very confident)

- How to pray and speak with God in a meaningful way:

1	2	3	4	5	6	7	8	9	10

(Not confident)   (Very confident)

- How to know God's will:

1	2	3	4	5	6	7	8	9	10

(Not confident)   (Very confident)

- How to deal with temptation and the reality of sin:

1	2	3	4	5	6	7	8	9	10

(Not confident)   (Very confident)

Have you been especially motivated to study or teach the Bible? If so, when?

How can you make time this week to continue growing in your knowledge of God and His Word?

What steps can you take to counter or reject false teaching in your community?

Responsive Prayer: *Lord Jesus, by the power of Your Name, I renounce Satan. Through the power of Your blood that was shed on the cross, I reject Satan's plans for my life and for my family. I ask You to fill me with Your Spirit so that I may always speak what is true and live as an example of what it truly means to follow You. Amen.*

NOTE
1. Jacques Godechot, "Napoleon I," *Britannica*, accessed July 29, 2021, https://www.britannica.com/biography/Napoleon-I.

MIDNIGHT

The Great White Throne

Then I saw a great white throne and Him who sat on it, from whose face the earth and the heaven fled away. And there was found no place for them. And I saw the dead, small and great, standing before God, and books were opened. And another book was opened, which is the Book of Life.

Revelation 20:11–12

There will be no future judgments after the Great White Throne Judgment. Death and hell will be finished, eternity will commence. We will all spend eternity somewhere—where will you be?

From Chapter 11 of *The End of the Age*

"New Jersey Woman Locked in 7-Year Battle With IRS to Prove She Is, Indeed, Alive." The headline grabbed the attention of thousands of people across the nation. Curious to learn more, they clicked on the news link and read the partly humorous—and partly horrifying—story of Samantha Dreissig.

According to the report, Samantha is a boisterous and energetic young woman. She is twenty-five years old. She lives with her father and works as a camp counselor during summers—an occupation that requires quite a lot of vim, vigor, and vitality. Despite these realities, the Internal Revenue Service is convinced that Samantha Dreissig is *dead*. The trouble began when Samantha's mother passed away of ovarian cancer in 2014. It was a difficult time for the family, but Samantha encountered another layer of difficulty when she attempted to file her taxes that same year. The IRS flagged the claim, declaring the filer to be deceased.

The simple explanation is that the IRS confused Samantha Dreissig with her mother—an error that is hard to explain when you realize neither women share the same first name or last name. Still, even understanding the root of the problem has not helped Samantha find a solution. She has endured hours of phone conversations. She has filed complaints. She even managed to wrangle a face-to-face meeting with an agent.

Seven years later, none of it worked. The last person she spoke with told her, "Wow, you're dead all over our system." Even worse, the problem is spreading! Samantha's father recently saw his tax return rejected. The reason? The IRS said that he was attempting to claim a deceased person as a dependent.[1]

All I can say is thank God that He keeps better records than the IRS!

As we reach the End of the Age, humanity will encounter a heavenly accounting system—one created by Christ Himself, Who is the ultimate Judge. Fortunately, Jesus will infinitely be more accurate than the bureaucrats running our world today. During that moment of reckoning, His divine books will be opened, and all things revealed. Alas, there will be no customer service number to call for those whose names are absent from the Book of Life. There will be no manager to which we can complain. All judgments are final.

Explore the Scripture

It has become popular in recent decades for Christian leaders to openly question the reality of hell. Pastors have preached sermons and written books emphasizing

God's love and relegating hell to a symbol or an empty threat. A majority of Americans believe that hell does not exist as a literal, physical place. Sadly, more and more Christians are adopting the same view.

In some ways, we can empathize with these opinions. It would be wonderful if there were no such thing as hell—no such thing as eternal punishment! The idea of even one person suffering such a fate for all of eternity is difficult to bear . . . let alone billions. But there's just one problem: the Bible declares regularly and unequivocally that hell is *real*. That hell exists. And that hell will be the eternal destination for any and all people who turn their backs on the free gift of salvation offered by Jesus.

Jesus believed in hell, for example:

[42] *"But whoever causes one of these little ones who believe in Me to stumble, it would be better for him if a millstone were hung around his neck, and he were thrown into the sea.* [43] *If your hand causes you to sin, cut it off. It is better for you to enter into life maimed, rather than having two hands, to go to hell, into the fire that shall never be quenched—* [44] *where*

> *'Their worm does not die
> And the fire is not quenched.'*

[45] *And if your foot causes you to sin, cut it off. It is better for you to enter life lame, rather than having two feet, to be cast into hell, into the fire that shall never be quenched—* [46] *where*

> *'Their worm does not die
> And the fire is not quenched.'*

[47] *And if your eye causes you to sin, pluck it out. It is better for you to enter the kingdom of God with one eye, rather than having two eyes, to be cast into hell fire—* [48] *where*

> *'Their worm does not die
> And the fire is not quenched.'"*

(MARK 9:42–48)

The apostle Paul believed in hell, which is why he wrote these passages:

> *⁶ Since it is a righteous thing with God to repay with tribulation those who trouble you, ⁷ and to give you who are troubled rest with us when the Lord Jesus is revealed from heaven with His mighty angels, ⁸ in flaming fire taking vengeance on those who do not know God, and on those who do not obey the gospel of our Lord Jesus Christ. ⁹ These shall be punished with everlasting destruction from the presence of the Lord and from the glory of His power, ¹⁰ when He comes, in that Day, to be glorified in His saints and to be admired among all those who believe, because our testimony among you was believed.*

> (2 THESSALONIANS 1:6–10)

And the apostle Peter revealed his belief in hell when he wrote:

> *⁴ For if God did not spare the angels who sinned, but cast them down to hell and delivered them into chains of darkness, to be reserved for judgment; ⁵ and did not spare the ancient world, but saved Noah, one of eight people, a preacher of righteousness, bringing in the flood on the world of the ungodly; ⁶ and turning the cities of Sodom and Gomorrah into ashes, condemned them to destruction, making them an example to those who afterward would live ungodly; ⁷ and delivered righteous Lot, who was oppressed by the filthy conduct of the wicked ⁸ (for that righteous man, dwelling among them, tormented his righteous soul from day to day by seeing and hearing their lawless deeds)— ⁹ then the Lord knows how to deliver the godly out of temptations and to reserve the unjust under punishment for the day of judgment.*

> (2 PETER 2:4–9)

What strikes you as most upsetting or provoking about these verses? Why?

What specifics were revealed about hell by each of these speakers?

- Jesus:

- Paul:

- Peter:

How should we understand the imagery connected to hell throughout the Bible?

What other Scripture verses or biblical evidence comes to mind as evidence for the existence of hell?

It's important for all Christians to know and believe that hell is literal place. That is the truth expressed in God's Word, and that truth will not change simply because it is inconvenient, or politically incorrect. At the same time, it's also important for Christians to understand that hell—sometimes referred to in Scripture as

Sheol or Hades—is not a permanent destination. Hell is a waiting place for the lost who must face judgment at the Great White Throne

This is why Peter noted in the passage above that angels are chained in hell in order "to be reserved for judgment." Final judgment comes *after* hell. Specifically, that final judgment will occur after the Millennium and after Satan, his army, and the Earth itself are destroyed by fire in the final battle of good against evil. Once those events have passed, Christ will sit in judgment and pass a final verdict over all who denied Him. The prophet Daniel was given a vision of that judgment:

> [9] *"I watched till thrones were put in place,*
> *And the Ancient of Days was seated;*
> *His garment was white as snow,*
> *And the hair of His head was like pure wool.*
> *His throne was a fiery flame,*
> *Its wheels a burning fire;*
> [10] *A fiery stream issued*
> *And came forth from before Him.*
> *A thousand thousands ministered to Him;*
> *Ten thousand times ten thousand stood before Him.*
> *The court was seated,*
> *And the books were opened.*

(DANIEL 7:9–10)

The apostle John recorded a similar vision in the book of Revelation:

> [11] *Then I saw a great white throne and Him who sat on it, from whose face the earth and the heaven fled away. And there was found no place for them.* [12] *And I saw the dead, small and great, standing before God, and books were opened. And another book was opened, which is the Book of Life. And the dead were judged according to their works, by the things which were written in the books.* [13] *The sea gave up the dead who were in it, and Death and Hades delivered up the dead who were in them. And they were judged, each one according to his works.* [14] *Then Death and Hades were cast into the lake of fire. This is the second death.* [15] *And anyone not found written in the Book of Life was cast into the lake of fire.*

(REVELATION 20:11–15)

What are some of the key images from these two passages?

What can you learn about Christ from each of these visions?

How would you summarize the "lake of fire"?

How should we understand the word *works* in Revelation 20:12?

In Revelation 20:14, John describes Death and Hades being cast into the lake of fire. What does that mean?

Reflect on the Scripture

The Great White Throne Judgment referred to by Daniel and John is one of seven imminent judgments that will take place at the End of the Age. The other six judgments are as follows:

1. The judgment seat of Christ, which will take place after the Rapture. Here, every believer from the Day of Pentecost to the Rapture will stand before Christ and be rewarded in heaven for their deeds done on earth (see 2 Corinthians 5:10).

2. The judgment of the Tribulation believer will occur at the end of the Tribulation. Those believers who were martyred for their faith in Christ during the Tribulation will be rewarded at this time (see Revelation 20:4–6).

3. The judgment of the Old Testament believers relates to those who will be resurrected and rewarded after the Second Coming (see Daniel 12:1–3).

4. The judgment of the Jews who survived the Tribulation. They will be judged after the Second Coming (see Ezekiel 20:34–38).

5. The judgment of the Gentile nations, also known as the judgment of the "sheep and the goats," will be based on how the Gentiles treated Israel and the Jewish people throughout the ages (see Matthew 25:31–46).

6. The judgment of Satan and his fallen angels takes place at the "judgment of the great day," will occur after the Millennial Kingdom (see Matthew 25:41; 2 Peter 2:4; Jude 6).

The final judgment is the Great White Throne Judgment of Revelation 20:11–15. This judgment will occur after Satan is thrown into the lake of fire. All the unjust people who have not been previously judged will come before the Lord and be adjudicated according to their evil works (see Acts 24:15). Like Satan and his angels, they will be sentenced to the lake of fire forever.

Notice that God has two sets of books. The Book of Life contains the name of every person who accepted Jesus Christ as Lord while they were on the earth.

When the wicked dead approach the Great White Throne, Jesus will first look for their names in the Book of Life. Obviously, they will not be recorded there. Next, He will open the books that contain His written records of every word, thought, and deed of the wicked. The result? "Anyone not found written in the Book of Life was cast into the lake of fire" (Revelation 20:15).

How would you describe or define the word *judgment*?

What does judgment mean in the context of the End of the Age?

Why is Jesus qualified to stand as Judge over humanity at this moment of the Great White Throne?

How have your beliefs about judgment and hell changed or evolved throughout your lifetime?

Act in Faith

Perhaps you are feeling a bit uncomfortable as you come to the end of this lesson. Hell is certainly a difficult subject to contemplate. It can also be a difficult idea to explain. This is why the discipline of apologetics is helpful for modern followers of Jesus—including individuals and the Church as a whole.

The Greek word *apologia* means "a reasoned defense." Those who study apologetics are thus simply preparing themselves to make a reasonable defense of their beliefs—the core doctrines of the Christian faith. Apologists offer a vital service to the Church by tackling difficult or confusing subjects in a way that makes them more understandable and teachable for laypersons.

In that spirit, let's conclude this lesson by engaging in some apologetic exercises regarding the biblical doctrines of hell and judgment.

How would you respond to someone who claims that hell is not a real place? What support from Scripture would you use to back up your reasoning?

Where do you see judgment being practiced in today's world? (Where do you see people being accused, tried, and punished for violating the world's standards?)

What does it look like for judgment to be carried out fairly?

What does it look like for judgment to be carried out unfairly?

What are the consequences of choosing not to exercise judgment or punishment within the following social circles:

- Families:

- The workplace:

- The legal system:

How would you respond to someone who said "it's not fair" for God to judge people for their unconfessed sins or send people to hell for eternity?

Responsive Prayer: *Lord God, I affirm that You alone are Judge over this universe. You alone are Judge over all people. Heavenly Father, I declare that I trust in Your goodness, mercy, love, and justice. Please guide me this week to follow Your will, speak boldly about Your Word, and act in ways that advance Your kingdom. Amen.*

NOTE

1. Jessica Layton, "New Jersey Woman Locked In 7-Year Battle With IRS To Prove She Is, Indeed, Alive," *CBS New York* (July 15, 2021), https://newyork.cbslocal.com/2021/07/15/woman-declared-dead-by-internal-revenue-service-samantha-dreissig/.

ETERNITY

Heaven and Earth Reborn

Behold, I create new heavens and a new earth; and the former shall not be remembered or come to mind. But be glad and rejoice forever in what I create; for behold, I create Jerusalem as a rejoicing, and her people a joy.

Isaiah 65:17–18

God will present us with a new heaven and a new earth. . . . We will be able to talk with God in the cool of the day as Adam did. The sinlessness of Eden will be recreated on earth, and in immortal bodies we will enjoy fellowship with God forever.

From Chapter 12 of *The End of the Age*

Today, it's possible to visit various cities that have impressed the world for centuries. Jerusalem, Paris, London, New York, Tokyo, Rome, Cairo, Mumbai, Caracas, Venice, Istanbul, Moscow, Beijing . . . the list goes on and on. However, there is one city that has captivated the world stage in recent decades. It's a city known for golden splendor and architectural marvels. I am talking about the city of Dubai.

Located on the Persian Gulf within the United Arab Emirates, Dubai has exploded in the last fifty years from a small fishing village to one of the most modern and impressive cities on our planet. Here are a few interesting facts about Dubai:

- Dubai has no income tax for its residents—not for individuals, and not even for companies operating within its borders.

- Residents of Dubai can earn a gram of gold for every kilogram of weight they lose in the pursuit of a healthier lifestyle.

- The world's only seven-star resort, the Burj-al-Arab, which is also the tallest building in the world is in Dubai.

- Dubai also has the world's largest garden, with millions of flowers spread over 72,000 square meters.[1]

From an architectural standpoint, Dubai represents the best of what modern man can achieve. However, with that in mind, can you imagine the glory and splendor of a city uniquely designed and specially crafted by God? The New Jerusalem will be magnificent beyond anything we could ever fathom!

Explore the Scripture

As we've seen throughout this study, the Old Testaments Scriptures have a great many things to say about the End of the Age. These prophecies are focused on what the apostle Paul called "perilous times" (2 Timothy 3:1)—including the overall degradation of society leading up the End of the Age, the Tribulation, Armageddon, the final conflict between God and Satan, and so on.

Yet there are Scripture passages and prophecies that point toward the hope and glory of our eternal destiny as citizens of heaven. And what a wonderful destiny it is! Look, for example, at what God revealed through the prophet Isaiah:

> [17] *"For behold, I create new heavens and a new earth;*
> *And the former shall not be remembered or come to mind.*
> [18] *But be glad and rejoice forever in what I create;*
> *For behold, I create Jerusalem as a rejoicing,*
> *And her people a joy.*
> [19] *I will rejoice in Jerusalem,*
> *And joy in My people;*
> *The voice of weeping shall no longer be heard in her,*
> *Nor the voice of crying.*
>
> [20] *"No more shall an infant from there live but a few days,*
> *Nor an old man who has not fulfilled his days;*
> *For the child shall die one hundred years old,*
> *But the sinner being one hundred years old shall be accursed.*
> [21] *They shall build houses and inhabit them;*
> *They shall plant vineyards and eat their fruit.*
> [22] *They shall not build and another inhabit;*
> *They shall not plant and another eat;*
> *For as the days of a tree, so shall be the days of My people,*
> *And My elect shall long enjoy the work of their hands.*
> [23] *They shall not labor in vain,*
> *Nor bring forth children for trouble;*
> *For they shall be the descendants of the blessed of the Lord,*
> *And their offspring with them.*
>
> [24] *"It shall come to pass*
> *That before they call, I will answer;*
> *And while they are still speaking, I will hear.*
> [25] *The wolf and the lamb shall feed together,*
> *The lion shall eat straw like the ox,*
> *And dust shall be the serpent's food.*

They shall not hurt nor destroy in all My holy mountain,"
Says the Lord.

(ISAIAH 65:17–25)

What strikes you as especially hopeful from this passage? Why?

What are some specific emotions referred to in these verses?

What are some specific promises contained in this passage?

How do these promises connect with your hopes and dreams for the future?

Our best glimpse of the glories to come in our heavenly home, including the New Jerusalem, are contained in the vision given to John the Revelator. After witnessing the devastating glimpses of the Tribulation and the final wars that will mark the end of the world as we know it, John received a beautiful picture of what life will be like in our eternal home:

> [1] *Now I saw a new heaven and a new earth, for the first heaven and the first earth had passed away. Also there was no more sea.* [2] *Then I, John, saw the holy city, New Jerusalem, coming down out of heaven from God, prepared as a bride adorned for her husband.* [3] *And I heard a loud voice from heaven saying, "Behold, the tabernacle of God is with men, and He will dwell with them, and they shall be His people. God Himself will be with them and be their God.* [4] *And God will wipe away every tear from their eyes; there shall be no more death, nor sorrow, nor crying. There shall be no more pain, for the former things have passed away."*
>
> [5] *Then He who sat on the throne said, "Behold, I make all things new." And He said to me, "Write, for these words are true and faithful."* . . .
>
> [9] *Then one of the seven angels who had the seven bowls filled with the seven last plagues came to me and talked with me, saying, "Come, I will show you the bride, the Lamb's wife."* [10] *And he carried me away in the Spirit to a great and high mountain, and showed me the great city, the holy Jerusalem, descending out of heaven from God,* [11] *having the glory of God. Her light was like a most precious stone, like a jasper stone, clear as crystal.* [12] *Also she had a great and high wall with twelve gates, and twelve angels at the gates, and names written on them, which are the names of the twelve tribes of the children of Israel:* [13] *three gates on the east, three gates on the north, three gates on the south, and three gates on the west.*
>
> [14] *Now the wall of the city had twelve foundations, and on them were the names of the twelve apostles of the Lamb.* [15] *And he who talked with me had a gold reed to measure the city, its gates, and its wall.* [16] *The city is laid out as a square; its length is as great as its breadth. And he measured the city with the reed: twelve thousand furlongs. Its length, breadth, and height are equal.* [17] *Then he measured its wall: one hundred and forty-four cubits, according to the measure of a man, that is, of an angel.* [18] *The construction of its wall was of jasper; and the city was pure gold, like clear glass.* [19] *The foundations of the wall of the city were adorned with all kinds of precious stones: the first foundation was jasper, the second sapphire, the third chalcedony, the fourth emerald,* [20] *the fifth sardonyx, the sixth sardius,*

the seventh chrysolite, the eighth beryl, the ninth topaz, the tenth chrysoprase, the eleventh jacinth, and the twelfth amethyst. [21] *The twelve gates were twelve pearls: each individual gate was of one pearl. And the street of the city was pure gold, like transparent glass.*

(REVELATION 21:1–5, 9–21)

Which of the pictures painted in these verses makes you most excited? Why?

Why is it significant that "God is with men, and He will dwell with them, and they shall be His people" (verse 3)?

Based on verses 9–21, how would you describe the New Jerusalem? What will it look like? What will it "feel" like from an emotional and relational perspective?

Look also at these rich promises from the final chapter in God's Word:

[1] *And he showed me a pure river of water of life, clear as crystal, proceeding from the throne of God and of the Lamb.* [2] *In the middle of its street, and on either side of the river, was the tree of life, which bore twelve fruits, each tree yielding its fruit*

every month. The leaves of the tree were for the healing of the nations. [3] And there shall be no more curse, but the throne of God and of the Lamb shall be in it, and His servants shall serve Him. [4] They shall see His face, and His name shall be on their foreheads. [5] There shall be no night there: They need no lamp nor light of the sun, for the Lord God gives them light. And they shall reign forever and ever.

(REVELATION 22:1–5)

What do you like best about these verses? Why?

How would you describe the significance of these promises:

- The presence of the tree of life with its twelve fruits

- God's throne and the Lamb in the midst of the people

- No more night—no more sun or lamps

Reflect on the Scripture

One of the core truths we must acknowledge from these passages of Scripture is that heaven is a *real place*. It is not a fantasy, nor symbolic or even a state of mind. Heaven is real—and it is our future home.

Jesus came from heaven to earth and then returned to heaven where He awaits the day when His Church shall join Him in the mansions He has prepared for His own. Jesus called heaven a "house . . . [with] many dwelling places" (John 14:2 NRSV). Heaven is not an illusion. It's just as real as the home in which you live right now.

In Acts 1:11, the angel told the disciples, "Men of Galilee, why do you stand gazing up into heaven? This same Jesus, who was taken up from you into heaven, will so come in like manner as you saw Him go into heaven." Did Jesus go up into a state of mind? Did He enter an abstraction? No! Jesus went to a real place, an eternal home, a place of perfection God has prepared as a place of reward for those who love Him.

Our citizenship lies in heaven. Paul wrote, "For our citizenship is in heaven, from which we also eagerly wait for the Savior, the Lord Jesus Christ" (Philippians 3:20). Our names are written in heaven. Jesus said, "Nevertheless do not rejoice in this, that the spirits are subject to you, but rather rejoice because your names are written in heaven" (Luke 10:20). And our treasures are stored in heaven. As Jesus also stated, "Do not lay up for yourselves treasures on earth . . . but lay up for yourselves treasures in heaven, where neither moth nor rust destroys and where thieves do not break in and steal" (Matthew 6:19–20).

The reality of heaven leads to another point worth remembering: our heavenly home will be a place of joy and purpose, not a life of idleness or boredom. We're not going to sit around heaven plucking harps all day. The truth is that heaven will be a place filled with fellowship and relationships—connection between ourselves and God, yes, but also deep and meaningful connection with other people. Not only will we know one another, but we will also be able to talk to the Old Testament saints, the prophets, Adam and Eve, the apostles, and the Lord Jesus Himself (see Hebrews 11).

Heaven will also be a place of incredible discovery. If you enjoy learning new things, exploring new worlds, and visiting new places, then heaven will be the perfect place for you. Imagine being able to fly to new planets where no man has gone before or exploring a new continent on the new earth. Best of all, we will learn about God, about our Savior, and about His plan for us. The Holy Scriptures will come together in our minds, and all mysteries will be revealed.

Heaven will be a place of work. When God set Adam and Eve in the Garden of Eden, He did not encourage them to languish about and nibble on some fruit every now and again. No, He blessed humanity with purpose, with meaningful work, with stewardship, and with goals and tasks to achieve. The same will be true in the city of our heavenly home.

Finally, yes, heaven will be a place bursting with praise and worship toward God. We will live in a state of constant gratitude and joy for all that God has achieved—and all the blessings we have received. Our opportunities to express that gratitude and joy will never end (see Isaiah 44:23; Revelation 14:3; 15:3).

What pictures or scenes form in your mind when you contemplate the reality of heaven?

What are you most looking forward to about your future heavenly home? Why?

How might your heavenly reality be different than your earthly experience in these key areas of life?

- Family:

- Work:

- Spiritual life:

What evidence can you point to in support of the claim that heaven is a real destination rather than a symbol or state of mind?

Act in Faith

God's Word is filled with many commands, all of which are essential for those who choose to follow Him. Yet one of the most important mandates found in all of Scripture is also one of the shortest. You can boil it down to just two words: "fear not." Again and again throughout the pages of the Bible, God tells His people not to fear. Why? Because fear is a byproduct of sin, which is rebellion against God by choosing to trust in ourselves or our circumstances rather than His power. This is why our world today is in such a chaotic state filled with fear and uncertainty.

The reality is that either we will conquer fear, or fear will conquer us. God gave us a wealth of prophecy in Scripture so that we could know what the future holds and *fear not*. For instance, we have seen that God wanted Daniel to look into the future and be assured. When it came time for that mighty prophet to die, we can be sure he laid down on his Babylonian couch, wrapped his cloak about him, and closed his eyes as if yielding to pleasant dreams. He knew he would see the God of Abraham face to face—the One in whom He had placed His trust.

Close this study by reading aloud the following verses from Psalm 118:

> [1] *Oh, give thanks to the LORD, for He is good!*
> *For His mercy endures forever.*
>
> [2] *Let Israel now say,*
> *"His mercy endures forever."*
> [3] *Let the house of Aaron now say,*
> *"His mercy endures forever."*

⁴ Let those who fear the Lord now say,
"His mercy endures forever."

⁵ I called on the Lord in distress;
The Lord answered me and set me in a broad place.
⁶ The Lord is on my side;
I will not fear.
What can man do to me?
⁷ The Lord is for me among those who help me;
Therefore I shall see my desire on those who hate me.
⁸ It is better to trust in the Lord
Than to put confidence in man.
⁹ It is better to trust in the Lord
Than to put confidence in princes. . . .

²⁹ Oh, give thanks to the Lord , for He is good!
For His mercy endures forever.

(PSALM 118:1–9, 29)

When have you felt uncertain or afraid while working through this study?

What steps can you take this week to conquer specific areas of fear in your life—especially fear of the future?

In what ways do the prophetic promises of the Bible offer hope and security?

What have you appreciated most from this study? Why?

What steps will you take in the coming weeks to adapt your life in the present so that you are more fully prepared for the End of the Age?

Responsive Prayer: *Lord God of Abraham, Isaac and Jacob, I affirm once again that You are fully sovereign and are fully in control of the past and the future. In every way possible, I place my trust in You, Lord Jesus. I trust You with my life now and throughout eternity. Amen.*

NOTE

1. Robin James, "23 Delightful Facts about Dubai," *FactCity* (June 19, 2020), https://factcity.com/facts-about-dubai/.

LEADER'S GUIDE

The following section is intended to give you some general structure and guidelines for going through the material in *The End of the Age* with a small group. If you're participating in a group study that has designated you as its leader, thank you for agreeing to serve in this capacity. What you have chosen to do is valuable and will make a great difference in the lives of others.

The End of the Age is a twelve-lesson study built around individual completion of this study guide and small-group interaction. As the group leader, just think of yourself as the host. Your job is to take care of your guests by managing all the behind-the-scenes details so that when everyone arrives, they can just enjoy time together.

As group leader, your role is not to answer all the questions or re-teach the content—the book, this study guide, and the Holy Spirit will do most of that work. Your job is to guide the experience and create an environment where people can process, question, and reflect—not receive more instruction.

Make sure everyone in the group gets a copy of the study guide. This will keep everyone on the same page and help the process run more smoothly. If some group members are unable to purchase the guide, arrange it so that people can share with other group members. Giving everyone access to all the material will position this study to be as rewarding an experience as possible. Everyone should feel free to write in their guides and bring them to group every week.

Setting Up the Group

As the group leader, you will want to create an environment that encourages sharing and learning. A church sanctuary or formal classroom may not be as ideal as a living room, because those locations can feel formal and less intimate. No matter what setting you choose, provide enough comfortable seating for everyone. This will make group interaction and conversation more efficient and natural.

Also, try to get to the meeting site early so that you can greet participants as they arrive. Simple refreshments create a welcoming atmosphere and can be a wonderful addition to a group study evening. Try to take food and pet allergies into account to make your guests as comfortable as possible. You may also want to consider offering childcare to those with children who want to attend. Managing these details up front will make the rest of your group experience flow smoothly and provide a welcoming space in which to engage the content of *The End of the Age*.

Starting Your Group Time

Once everyone has arrived, it's time to begin the group. Here are some simple tips to make your group time healthy, enjoyable, and effective.

First, consider beginning the meeting with a short prayer, and then remind the group members to put their phones on silent. This is a way to make sure you can all be present with one another and with God. Then, give each person one or two minutes to check in before diving into the material. In lesson one, participants can introduce themselves and share what they hope to experience in this group study. Beginning in lesson two, people may need more time to share their insights from their personal studies and to enjoy getting better acquainted.

As you begin going through the material, invite members to share their experiences and discuss their responses with the group. Usually, you won't answer the discussion questions yourself, but you may need to go first a couple of times and set an example, answering briefly and with a reasonable amount of transparency. You may also want to help participants debrief and process what they're learning as they complete each session individually ahead of each group meeting. Debriefing something like this is a bit different from responding to questions about the material because the content comes from their real lives. The basic experiences that you want the group to reflect on are:

- *What was the best part about this week's individual study?*
- *What was the hardest part?*
- *What did I learn about myself?*
- *What did I learn about God?*

Leading the Discussion Time

Encourage all the group members to participate in the discussion, but make sure they know they don't have to do so. As the discussion progresses, you may want to follow up with comments such as, "Tell me more about that," or, "Why did you answer that way?" This will allow the group participants to deepen their reflections and invite meaningful sharing in a nonthreatening way.

While each session in this study guide includes multiple sections, you do not have to go through each section and cover every question or exercise. Feel free to go with the dynamic in the group and skip around if needed to cover all the material more naturally. You can pick and choose questions based on either the needs of your group or how the conversation is flowing. Also, don't be afraid of silence. Offering a question and allowing up to thirty seconds of silence is okay. It allows people space to think about how they want to respond and also gives them time to do so.

As group leader, you are the boundary keeper for your group. Do not let anyone (yourself included) dominate the group time. Keep an eye out for group members who might be tempted to "attack" those they disagree with or try to "fix" those having struggles. These kinds of behaviors can derail a group's momentum, so they need to be steered in a different direction. Model active listening and encourage everyone in your group to do the same. This will make your group time a safe space and create a positive community.

At the end of each group session, you may want to encourage the participants to take just a few minutes to review what they've learned and write down one or two key takeaways. This will help them cement the big ideas in their minds as you close the session. Close your time together with prayer as a group.

Thank you again for taking the time to lead your group. You are making a difference in the lives of others and having an impact on the kingdom of God.

ABOUT THE AUTHOR

John Hagee is the founder and senior pastor of Cornerstone Church in San Antonio, Texas, a nondenominational evangelical church with more than 22,000 active members. He is the author of more than forty books including several *New York Times* bestsellers, his latest being *Earth's Last Empire: The Final Game of Thrones*. Pastor Hagee is the founder and chairman of Christians United for Israel (CUFI) with more than ten million members. Hagee Ministries television and radio outreach spans America and the nations of the world.

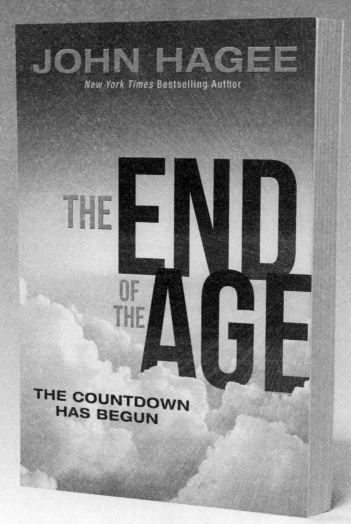